ONLY THE BEST WILL DO

NOEL DAVIDSON

AMBASSADOR

BELFAST ◆ **GREENVILLE**
NORTHERN IRELAND   SOUTH CAROLINA

ONLY THE BEST WILL DO
Copyright © 1998 Noel Davidson

First published November 1998
Reprinted December 1998

ISBN 1 84030 043 4

Ambassador Publications
a division of
Ambassador Productions Ltd.
Providence House
Ardenlee Street,
Belfast,
BT6 8QJ
Northern Ireland
www.ambassador-productions.com

Emerald House
427 Wade Hampton Blvd.
Greenville
SC 29609, USA
www.emeraldhouse.com

CONTENTS

FOREWORD

❖

It is always a great pleasure to introduce two of your old friends to each other. It is particularly rewarding when it results in a book of considerable value.

Those who are well acquainted with Eddie Stobart can appreciate the reluctance of a man who is genuinely humble to have any form of publicity. Yet there was a great story lying behind what is now a household name in the United Kingdom.

I was so pleased that he was eventually persuaded that such a book would be an inspiration and example to others and could be used to the glory of his God.

This is really the story of two lives because Nora Stobart features prominently in this book as she has in the life of her husband. Having got to know both Eddie and Nora very well over the years I feel that Noel Davidson with his distinctive style has been able to convey something of their very special qualities. Once again he has been able to use his individual gift to good effect.

I am quite sure it is the desire of both the author and the subjects of this work that it will be used to influence others to enter into the great spiritual experience which has played the central part in Eddie Stobart's life and to encourage others who already have this certainty of salvation to a greater commitment.

Above all they would pray that it is used to the glory of the One who has 'done everything well' (Mark 7 v. 37)

Norman Mc Call
Larne, Co. Antrim.

October, 1998.

INTRODUCTION

❖

A s we were walking out of church together one Sunday, some eighteen months ago, my friend Norman Mc Call remarked to me, "Rosemary and I spent last weekend with a couple and his, indeed both of their life stories would make a terrific book."

"And who were they?" I enquired, always alert for a new subject for a biography. Especially one which was going to make 'a terrific book'.

"Eddie Stobart, and his wife Nora," Norman replied.

"Eddie Stobart. The name rings a bell," I reflected.

"Yes. Eddie is the man who founded the company, Eddie Stobart Ltd.. You see the lorries all over the place in England. Eddie is now retired, though, and his sons Edward and William operate the transport business," Norman went on to inform me. "Eddie and Nora are fine Christians and are involved in all kinds of Christian work. I have come to know them through the work of The Gideons."

I was interested.

It did seem to me, from what I had heard, that there was 'a terrific book' buried in there somewhere. Just waiting for someone to come along, dig it up, and write it!

A year ago this month, Norman and his wife Rosemary, arranged for my wife, Liz, and me, to meet Eddie and Nora.

On meeting them, I was impressed with Eddie and Nora straightaway. Impressed particularly by two things.

Their forthright honesty and their genuine humility.

Eddie calls 'a spade a spade'. Straight out. No beating about the bush. Both he and Nora have been very concerned during all our research that everything said, and then written, would be absolutely honest and fair. To everybody.

What impressed me most about this couple, though, was their unaffected humility. When I suggested that the story of their lives would make an interesting book their immediate and impulsive reaction was, "Who would want to read about us?"

I laughed.

Here were a couple who had, in their lifetime, and in their own separate ways, made a tremendous impact both on the business world, and for God, and they had responded, eyes wide in astonishment, "Who would want to read about us?"!

How they each came to know the Lord, and then each other, is a touching love-story in itself!

Eddie had seen a very successful business built up from very humble beginnings. They had both been close friends of the well-known Bible teacher, Dr. Martyn Lloyd-Jones. They had helped establish a church in Wigton, their home town. Nora, herself, who was orphaned at the age of four, and had a most unhappy early childhood, was at that time National President of the Auxiliaries, the women's section of The Gideons.

Who would want to read about us, indeed?!

When I did eventually get around to convincing Eddie and Nora that a book about their lives would be a worthwhile project, it was only by pointing out to them that their story could be of help to others. It could, perhaps, even be instrumental in leading someone to know the Saviour, who meant so much to them. Eddie summed it up. Straight as ever. "If we agree to have this book written, it will be on one condition. That it is a book which gives glory to God, and not Eddie Stobart. For I am nobody, you know. Just a farmer's lad, whom God has blessed."

INTRODUCTION

Having agreed to fulfil Eddie's 'one condition', I began to research the book. It has been a happy task. We have had many meetings and telephone calls. One has to. To touch the soul of the subject(s).

When Liz, my constant companion and counsellor, and I, arrived for the first time to stay with Eddie and Nora in their lovely home in the Cumbrian countryside, on the outskirts of a rural village, I was reminded of Thomas Gray's oft-quoted words from his 'Elegy Written In A Country Churchyard', describing the sincere and unassuming folk amongst whom he lived:-

Far from the madding crowd's ignoble strife,
Their sober wishes never learnt to stray,
Along the cool sequestered vale of life,
They kept the noiseless tenor of their way.'

Eddie and Nora exactly. People who love God. And the quiet country way of life. They had tried the city, having lived for six years in Carlisle, but they couldn't settle there. They yearned for the country and returned to it. Now, in retirement, they seem to travel more than ever to undertake a variety of Christian engagements. But their chief delight is to return to their village haven. The flowers in the garden at the front, a herd of cows in a field at the back, a variety of trees all around. And 'the peace of God which passes all understanding' over all...

Over the past year I have come to know Eddie and Nora Stobart very well. It is impossible to write a comprehensive biography and not know the subjects very well. It goes farther than that, however.

A few months ago Eddie and Nora came over to Northern Ireland to stay at our home. To allow me the opportunity for some more in-depth research. As Liz and I were preparing to say our 'Good-byes' to them at the end of their stay, Eddie said something very significant. "I can see that we are doing more than writing a book here," he remarked. "We are making new friends."

So we now consider ourselves greatly enriched to class Eddie and Nora amongst our friends.

I trust that as you read this book you will come to consider them as your friends, too. For that is what they would love to be. And that is the kind of people they are. Normal, warm and friendly.

Above and beyond that, though, everyone involved in the production of this book has one specific desire, and it is this. That you may come to a much deeper appreciation of Eddie and Nora's God, the One who can do for you what He has done for them. Change your life when you come to Him and bless your life as you trust in Him.

Noel I. Davidson.
October, 1998.

1

I AM A LITTLE SOLDIER

❖

"I am a little soldier,
I'm only four years old,
I mean to fight for Jesus,
And wear a crown of gold."

It was April, 1934. The audience at the packed-out, crammed-in, Sunday School social in the tiny Methodist Church in Hesket Newmarket, Cumbria, listened intently, and his parents glowed with pride, as little Eddie Stobart, who was 'only four years old', made his first public appearance. Saying his 'recitation'.

Eddie's parents were Christians whose prime concern for their firstborn son was that he should trust in, and then live for, Jesus. So they sent him along each week to the Sunday School at the village Methodist Church, where they were members. At that Sunday School, godly teachers taught the little ones the Bible stories, and encouraged them to learn Scripture verses. When still very young, Eddie was presented with a special prize for learning, and reciting, 'without a mistake', Psalm 51 v.10. 'Create in me a clean heart , O God ; and renew a right spirit within me'.

Later on in 1934, in August, Eddie's education took another step forward. He started 'day' school. As the schoolteacher was a close friend of his mother's, Eddie was collected and taken to school every morning in Mary's Austin Seven. It was great to ride along in the car, when most of the other children at the school had to trudge there on foot. Especially on wet days. But it had its disadvantages, too. Eddie didn't like to be considered 'the teacher's pet'. And he could never ever bring himself to call his teacher, 'Miss'. She had always been plain 'Mary', to him. After all, his mammy didn't call her 'Miss'. Why should he?

Out of school, there were two activities that took up a lot of the growing boy's time. And neither of these was homework. Eddie hadn't a lot of time for that kind of thing. He did what he had to do. What he was forced to do. But no more. That was all. He had far too many other far more important things crowding his days.

One of the two activities which occupied most of his out-of-school waking hours was an expected occupation. He performed these duties because they were part of his daily routine.

The other was a pleasant diversion. Took him away from that very daily routine. So he did it because he enjoyed it.

The first was his involvement with the work on the farm. The second was his attendance at little Methodist 'chapels', dotted all around the surrounding countryside, with his dad, who was a lay-preacher.

The Stobart farm, called Bankdale Head, near Hesket Newmarket, was a thirty-two acre holding. It was a 'mixed farm' in every true sense of the word!

The land was worked with horses, and the strong young lad soon learnt to handle a team, trained by his father, who was an expert. There were stalls for eight cows, which had to be milked, morning and evening. Every day. And again, the-son-on-the-farm was expected to help with the milking. Then the cream had to be 'separated' and left in cans at the farm gate. To be collected by Carrick's Creamery cart. Every day.

No mixed farm would be complete without its poultry. The Stobarts kept nearly three hundred hens. So the eggs had to be collected, and cleaned. Every day. Then they were packed into boxes, and left at the farm gate, once a week. To be collected by the man from the Express Diary. When he had loaded the eggs on to his cart he left the previous week's payment in an empty crate.

Country people must be honest people, surely!

And just to ensure that their 'mixed farm' was truly 'mixed', John Stobart, Eddie's dad, reared a bull every year. This young bull was kept on the farm for a dual purpose. When he was fully reared he was sold, and his selling price looked after the annual farm rent. And for the duration of his stay at Bankdale Head he cleaned up the most of the skimmed milk from 'the separator'!

Times were tough. The work was hard. And constant. And profits weren't big.

But the young Eddie Stobart grew up in a happy, stable home.

His parents were blissfully content.

Their faith was in God.

One of the benefits of having a mixed farm was that you could almost live off it. Eggs and milk. Home-made bread. And butter. Potatoes. A pig for bacon now and again, and a rooster for the Christmas table. It was, in effect, 'subsistence farming'.

'Addie' (Adelaide) Stobart, Eddie's mother, kept the books. Meticulously. Every penny of income and expenditure was accounted for in her neat handwriting.

Once, when she had balanced the books at the end of a year's really hard, nose-to-the-grindstone work, Eddie heard her telling his father, with some satisfaction that they had made five pounds that year. Five pounds! Total annual profit, after tax! Five pounds!

This, however, was considered good. Many of their neighbours had worked extremely hard, as well, but had failed to break even.

John and Addie just praised God for His goodness.

The diversion that Eddie enjoyed so much, away from the humdrum of eggs and milk, eggs and milk, of the farm, was to go for a ride with his father, on his motor-bike. When he was younger he sat on the petrol tank, with his father's protective arms around him. Then, when he grew too big for the petrol-tank, he sat on the saddle-bag at the back, clinging around his father's waist. And on trips around the farm, or down into the village, Gyp, the collie, took his place on the petrol tank. There he sat, his fur stuck out rigid in the wind, looking all around him.

John Stobart travelled many miles on his B.S.A.

On a summer afternoon he would leave the hayfield, and set off for the Keswick Convention, taking Eddie with him. This was a fascinating experience for the young boy from the farm.

The meetings in the massive tent were the only bits of the outing to Keswick that Eddie didn't really, deep-down-in-his-heart, enjoy. For two reasons. Firstly, the tent was enormous. And he was anything but enormous. So he often found himself stuck in the middle of a row, behind a big woman with an even bigger hat. So he couldn't see the speaker. Whoever, or wherever, he was.

Although he many a time couldn't see the preacher, he could always hear him. But that was no great boon either. For half the time he couldn't understand what the man was talking about.

However, his father seemed to appreciate it. And the most interesting time of every meeting for Eddie was when it was all over. As his father mingled with his many friends, reliving with them the 'marvellous ministry' and 'challenging messages', point by point, the young boy stayed close to him, for he dreaded getting lost in that crowd, but he wasn't listening to the men's conversations. He was looking around. And trying to listen to somebody else's...

That was the great thing about the Keswick Convention. You saw so many different kinds of people there. These visits to the Convention were the first lessons in Eddie Stobart's cultural education. There he saw people of many different nationalities. With different colours of skin. And ways of speaking.

It was the variety of languages that fascinated the pillion-passenger from Hesket Newmarket most of all. He used to like to sidle up beside them. To hear if they were saying 'funny' words. Very occasionally he was rewarded with an unintelligible to him, torrent of language, accompanied, as a bonus, with enthusiastic gesticulations. But mostly he was disappointed. Usually these people spoke very good English. Sometimes better than his own !

The week (as it was then), of the Keswick Convention, was the spiritual highlight of the year for John Stobart. But for the other fifty-one weeks he faithfully served God. As a Methodist lay-preacher. And Eddie enjoyed his seated-on-the-saddlebag trips, with his father to little Methodist Churches in the area around their home, sharing in the Cumberland country 'chapel' experience.

One night, before the service commenced, the chapel steward came up to Eddie's father, who was to be the visiting speaker, and whispered, "There is usually a time for prayer after this evening service. But forget about it tonight, for once. You see, there is only me that prays here. And I don't feel like praying tonight."

Eddie always remembered that man. And the knowing smile that creased around his father's lips as he agreed to remain silent about the praying. It was obvious that he understood the man's dilemma. There must have been times that he hadn't felt up to praying himself !

On another night, Eddie and his dad arrived at an isolated country chapel, to find it full. Nearly every available seat appeared to be taken. It was with some difficulty that they eventually found the preacher's junior travelling companion somewhere to sit. He ended up balancing precariously on the very end of a wooden bench. It was even worse than the saddle-bag of the motor-bike ! He didn't have his dad's waist to cling on to !

The service had started and John Stobart was in the pulpit. He had just begun his sermon when the chapel steward climbed the two steps and arrived up beside him. He turned up the wick of the Tilley lamp that overhung the reading desk. Then, deciding that the congregation needed more volume, as well as more light, he put his arm around the speaker's shoulder, and said into his ear, in a stage whisper, "Shout out man! We can't hear you. You are working for God, you know!"

John Stobart complied. He spoke a bit louder for the rest of the service. But he never forgot the chapel steward's advice, either. For the rest of his life.

It was a good motto for a Christian to live by.

If he was working for God, whether preaching the Gospel, teaching the Scriptures, or witnessing to friends and neighbours, then what he was saying was bound to be worth hearing.

So he would shout it out !

2

THE LAST MILE OF THE WAY

❖

Addie Stobart had always been a jolly sort of a person. A vibrant, radiant Christian who loved life. She used to laugh a lot. Enjoyed a joke.

Before Eddie's little brother, Ronnie, was born in 1936, John Stobart employed a maid to help his wife with the housework. And to look after the family.

With her husband out at work on the farm all day, and with Eddie either at school or out on the farm too, Addie appreciated the company of another lively, jovial woman. She and her helper used to spend many happy hours, sharing the daily chores.

Often when they were working together upstairs, changing a bed, perhaps, the clear ring of their laughter would echo around the house and out across the yard. Or when they were sitting sharing a welcome cup of tea by the fire, before embarking upon some other project, either one of the would tell quite a simple joke, or recall an amusing incident. Then both of them would collapse into howls of uncontrollable mirth!

On such occasions, when his mother was obviously so happy, it used to puzzle young Eddie when he heard his dad, who loved her dearly, rebuke her gently.

"Addie, if you don't stop laughing like that you will be 'aving an 'eart attack," he used to say, his amiable approach only faintly masking an air of anxiety.

Eddie wondered about all the talk of 'an 'eart attack', when he heard it so often. And then when his mother's health began to deteriorate he realized that his father had been genuinely concerned about her.

The bouncing, cheerful, rosy-cheeked woman who was his mother, gradually changed. She became slower in her movements. Less animated in her conversations. Paler in her complexion.

A painful discovery began to unfold in his boyish mind. An unwelcome understanding. Now that he was ten years of age, his mother wasn't by any means the same person that he had known when he was four. Or five. Or six.

She was ill. But he had no idea, yet, just how ill.

On Christmas Day, 1941, when Eddie was twelve years old, his mother was too weak to rise. Yet she dearly wanted her husband John, and her two boys to have some kind of a memorable Christmas Day. So she plied her older son with all kinds of instructions as to how to make the dinner. What to do. How, and when, to do it.

Eddie was growing up. Fast.

He had to.

When he was younger he used to watch his mother peeling potatoes. The knife moved so deftly. The potatoes turned in her hand so naturally. And the skin came off in one long curly spiral. It all seemed so easy. But as he sat that morning by his mother's bedside, trying to perform that simplest of kitchen tasks, he realized that it wasn't just as easy as it first appeared.

The potato stuck, like a stone, in his hand. He couldn't manage to get the skin to come off in one or two long pieces either. He was trying. Hard. And his mother was advising, and encouraging him, patiently. All he was managing to achieve, however, was to cut chunks off the potato. No matter what shape the potatoes were when they came into his hand, round, oblong, or all-odd-shaped, when Eddie was finished and they plopped into the basin of water at his feet, they were square! Every single one of them!

Then, unexpectedly, in the middle of the potato-peeling session, help arrived!

When he heard the sound of a car engine purring up into the yard Eddie dropped a half-peeled, half-square potato into the half-full basin and rushed over to the window.

Who could be calling with them on Christmas Day ? It certainly wouldn't be the man from the creamery. Or the egg-man. Who could it be ?

It was his older cousins, Zanna and Ruth Johnston, from Newhouse Farm, near Carlisle. In their Armstrong Siddeley. And when they came into the house, to deliver their presents, what cheer they brought to the young cook-in-training ! For as well as Christmas presents for all at Bankdale Haed, they also produced, from the innards of their lovely car, a half-cooked chicken. And bagfuls of prepared vegetables.

Eddie appreciated the personal sacrifice on his cousins' part. Leaving all the excitement of a big family on a Christmas morning, to drive ten miles. Just to be kind to them. To make sure they had everything they needed. And he was delighted with the provisions which they had brought. For two very practical reasons. His father, little five year old Ronnie and he all had an excellent Christmas dinner. And he didn't have to mutilate another single potato!

During the winter months that followed, dragging 1941 into 1942, Addie was occasionally able to be up and about. But she couldn't do much work. She wasn't able. She just sat around. Smiling. Advising. Encouraging. And playing the piano.

One of her favourite occupations during those weak and weary, winter days, was to sit down and allow her thinning fingers to float over the keys of the piano. She used to sit in the parlour, on a Sunday evening, when the family who had been out at church, returned, and play. And sing.

It was cosy.

The wind whistling around the windows of the farmhouse on the hillside. The logs on the fire fizzing and flaring and flaming. The soothing sound of the piano, sweetly played. And mother singing.

Her favourite piece, the one that she always sang, in every sitting-singing-session, was one that touched Eddie.

One that held comfort for his mother. But an unmistakable message for him.

One that assured her that she was approaching her heavenly home. And relief from pain and suffering. But it unsettled him. Twelve year-old 'big boys' didn't cry, or so he thought, so Eddie had often hastily to wipe away the tears that welled up in his eyes and threatened to spill over conspicuously down his cheeks, as he heard her sing softly...

If I walk in the pathway of duty,
If I work to the close of the day;
I shall see the great King in His beauty,
When I've gone the last mile of the way.

If for Christ I proclaim the glad story,
If I seek for His sheep gone astray,
I am sure he will show me His glory,
When I've gone the last mile of the way.

Here the dearest of ties we must sever,
Tears of sorrow are seen ev'ry day;
But no sickness, no sighing forever,
When I've gone the last mile of the way.

And if here I have earnestly striven,
And have tried all His will to obey,
'Twill enhance all the rapture of heaven,
When I've gone the last mile of the way.'

But it was the chorus that always stuck in young Eddie's mind. Repeated, as it was, four times in the course of the singing of the hymn. A hymn that talked about 'dearest ties' being severed. About 'no sickness, no sighing forever.'

It was the chorus that haunted him. On the way to school. In the henhouse. In the byre. In his bed. It always came whispering back in waves washing over his worried mind...

When I've gone the last mile of the way,
I will rest at the close of the day,
And I know there are joys that await me;
When I've gone the last mile of the way'.

During the spring of 1942, Addie Stobart spent spells of varying length in the City General Hospital, Carlisle. She knew that she wasn't going to get better. Each visit to the Hospital saw her weaker. Having less strength. And requiring more care and attention. But there was little that the medical profession could do for her now.

She was on the last lap of 'the last mile of the way.'

As a wife and mother she was concerned for her husband and her two boys. What would become of them when she was gone? Dying held no terrors for her. She was going to be with Christ. Of that she was sure.

Her only hope for her loved ones, was in God. In committing them into His all-powerful and all-tender care. This she did in prayer. Constantly.

On Friday, 19th June, 1942, Eddie's father told him that his mother wanted to see him.

When he went into the darkened bedroom, curtains pulled to subdue the dazzle of the summer sun, his mother beckoned for him to come over to the bedside. When he did so, the pale and pathetic figure reached out a trembling hand. It was obvious that she was wanting to hold Eddie's.

He placed his developing and by-now well-worked hand into hers, by-now so frail and feeble. And she held it. As strongly as her diminishing strength would permit.

Then she spoke. She had something that she wanted to say to her firstborn son. It was the final expression of her special ambition for her boy.

"Eddie," she began, still holding his hand, and looking intently up into his face, "I am going soon to live with the Lord Jesus. I want you to promise me that you will trust in Him and grow up to love Him."

"Yes, I will," Eddie replied, huskily. His voice, like the power in his legs, had left him.

But although he had promised his mother that he would 'love Jesus', his promise wasn't really from the heart at that moment. Nor after he left the room and for all the remainder of that declining summer day.

Pangs of bitterness sprang up within him.

Why does my mammy have to die? he asked himself.

My mammy loved Jesus and served him faithfully herself, he reasoned. Why does she have to be taken, when lots of women who have never even trusted in Jesus are all in good health?

Is it fair, leaving wee Ronnie and me without our mammy? he argued with himself.

A sullen, smouldering resentment possessed him.

But he wouldn't say anything to anybody. Everybody around him had quite enough to cope with at present. And anyway, who was there to talk to? The person with whom he had done by far the most of his talking, was lying in another room. Dying.

Next day, Saturday 20th June, at noon, Addie Stobart did what she had told Eddie that she was going to do. She went to live with Jesus. She passed peacefully away. She died.

When he heard of her death, Eddie stood on the stairs of Bankdale Head, gazing out through the distinctive arched window to the meadows that fell away from the farm. He was looking, but not seeing.

His mother had 'gone the last mile of the way'. And that was happy for her. She had gone to 'see the great King in His beauty' and experience 'the joys that' awaited her. Lovely. Great. He was glad that all her physical pain and misery were over.

But what about him?

He had been deprived of his mother.

At twelve. Coming thirteen.

And he still had many, many miles to go.

What was to become of him?

3

COW'S MILK, HORSE POWER AND RABBIT STEW

❖

fter his mother's death, young Eddie Stobart was compelled to take even more responsibility for the work on the farm. This annoyed him at first. He felt very emotionally unstable. And bitter. In a peculiar sense, on his own in the world, despite the best efforts of his father, relatives, and a short succession of housekeepers, to befriend and comfort him.

He wanted to be left alone, too. To be a boy. And grow up, slowly.

Not somebody who knew nothing else but going to school from Monday to Friday, to the Methodist chapel twice on a Sunday, and working on the farm nearly every other available daylight hour. And sometimes after dark as well.

But that's not the way it was. The work was there to be done.

Eddie was expected to do it.

So he did it.

Every morning, before setting out for school, he had to do the milking. Hand - milk the two cows. And not long after he returned in the afternoon he would have to go out and fetch those same two cows from the pasture, and tie them up in the byre. Where they stood patiently, waiting to be milked. Again.

In addition to taking on responsibility for the milking, Eddie started to work with the horses, in the summer of 1942. He was only thirteen years of age. But he loved the big gentle animals. Working with them became a source of solace to him. They were his friends. He could talk to them. And they didn't sicken him silly with all kinds of patronizing platitudes, either. They were just there for him when he needed them.

So he learnt how to harness them into a plough. Or a cart.

And how to handle them in a field. Or on the road.

He took responsibility for following the steadily plodding team as they pulled a plough or a harrow, up and down the fields, in the spring. Then, with those same horses he learnt how to mow the fields. In the summer and the autumn. First the hay. Then the corn.

The Second World War was raging across Europe during Eddie's teenage years, but it was far removed from the peace and tranquility of the Cumbrian fells. However, the war that brought hardship and death to so many, brought a strange sort of a bonus to the young son of a farmer. Since so many of Britain's menfolk were away from home, serving in the forces, all young lads of thirteen years of age and upwards, living in the country, were allowed time off school at busy periods of the year. To help work on the land.

Eddie was pleased about this. Maybe it was worthwhile being a farmer's boy after all. During the spring, with all the sowing and planting, and in the autumn, with its reaping and harvesting, he had a legitimate excuse for skipping school. It was great.

As his working on the land exemption didn't apply in high summer, Eddie went to school during the summer term of 1943. But he didn't mind though. He was one of the oldest in the whole school. And it was his last term. He would be leaving at the end of July.

On many of those hot and hazy summer days, Eddie had some unusual company on his way to school. When he was in 'senior infants' he had learnt a nursery rhyme about some girl called Mary whose little lamb 'followed her to school one day'... 'And all the children laughed to see, a little lamb at school.'

Since he was so busy, as a just-turned-fourteen year old, Eddie took, not his 'little lamb', but his two big horses, to school. And 'all the children' paid not the slightest bit of notice!

Rising early on many of those dewy summer mornings, Eddie did the milking, and then hitched his team up to the mowing machine. Then they would rumble down the road to a field of hay that neeeded to be cut. Either for his dad, or some other local farmer. Eddie and his team worked away in that field, as the world around them stirred itself into wakefulness.

When it came nearly nine o'clock, the three of them left the field, and rumbled on. Into Hesket Newmarket. There, in a field beside the school, Eddie unhitched the two horses, and left them to their own devices. While he went into the little building with all his schoolfriends. Boys through one door. Girls through another.

At morning break time and in the lunch hour, Eddie would check anxiously that his two companions, which hadn't followed him, but that he had driven, to school, were O.K. And they usually were. Either lying stretched out. Or up ambling about.

When the afternoon bell rang, Eddie packed up his schoolbooks and yoked up his horses, and went back to where he had left off in the morning. Either to finish the field he had begun, or to 'open up' another one somewhere else.

Then, when the evening shadows began to lengthen, the team of three would set off for Bankdale Head. Where the two cows would already be tied up in the byre. Patiently waiting. To be milked. Again.

When he left school at fourteen, two things happened in Eddie's life. Both of which helped to restore a sense of stability and self-esteem to the developing lad.

The first was that his father remarried. This was good, for at last Eddie had a mother-figure at home again. Ruth, the new Mrs. Stobart, was very kind to both he and Ronnie. And the two boys soon came to appreciate having someone who was considerate, and permanent, in the house to come home to. Always.

Times were hard. Money was scarce. It would take his father busy scraping a living for four of them again off the land. So the entrepreneurial Eddie, even at fourteen, decided that he was going to make himself a bit of extra money. To augment his allowance for working on the farm.

His plan was simple. He would trap rabbits. And sell them.

There was a War on. And fresh meat was scarce. So Eddie concluded that if he could only devise some way of catching even some of the multitude of rabbits that burrowed and scurried and nibbled away their days around Bankdale Head, he could find a market for them somewhere. It would always make 'a bob or two'.

Having acquired, or designed, an assortment of traps and snares, Eddie put his plan into action. It was worth a try, he reckoned. He placed his traps at strategic points all over the farm. At rabbit runs through hedges. At burrows in banks. And in the woods.

It worked, too. Soon he had a number of rabbits, strung up by the back legs in an outhouse. But they were no use to him in there. He needed to turn them into money. And fast. They weren't going to be fresh forever!

Where could he go to find sufficient housewives, to relieve him of his rabbits?

The answer to that one was simple, too. In Carlisle market.

Soon Eddie had a flourishing little sideline going. Trapping rabbits out on the farm. Then selling them for half-a-crown each in the market in Carlisle. He had no difficulty in finding buyers for them, either. Thrifty housewives soon got to know about 'the young lad from 'esket Newmarket who sells the rabbits'. And they would be waiting for him to arrive with his sacks of 'merchandise'. Queued up. If you had a big family to feed, and both money and meat were in short supply, there was a lot you could do with a good, fat, fresh rabbit. A big pot of rabbit stew would be a real treat for a couple of days!

The name and fame of Eddie-the-rabbit-catcher began to spread.

It wasn't long until neighbouring farmers were inviting him to rid their fields of the ravening rabbits. He did so, with the greatest of pleasure. It required constant commitment, on top of his every day duties for his father, but it brought in a constant income. And that was important.

A local farmer approached Eddie, one day, and said, "Eddie, I would like you to come over and 'take the rabbits' on my land. I don't think there will be very many, mind you. But you are welcome to take what you can."

When he began to 'work' that farm, the intrepid rabbit-hunter soon realized that the farmer's estimate of the numbers of rabbits on his farm had been wildly inaccurate. 'I don't think there will be very many', had been his forecast.

A number of carefully placed traps and snares across that man's fields yielded twelve dozen rabbits in a week! A gross!

That represented a gross of satisfied housewives in Carlisle market. With a gross of satisfied families with their bowls of rabbit stew.

And it also represented a gross of half-crowns for a satisfied, hard-working, trap-setting Eddie!

Just after his eldest son left school at fourteen, prospects became a little brighter for John Stobart, too. Financially, as well as romantically. It was then that he secured a contract with the County Council for the services of a horse and cart and man. The contract provided a welcome source of additional income for him. For the pay was good at £ 1 / 7 /6 (£1.35), per day. Only problem was though that the 'man' who drove the horse and cart on these contract jobs was not a man at all. The 'man' was a boy. Eddie.

So, with his days fully occupied, a bit of stability at home and a pound or two of his own, Eddie began to contemplate his next enterprise. He had another idea for putting the few pounds of savings which he had, plus some of his rabbit-money, to good use. He saw another business possibility...

Before his fifteeneth birthday he bought an 'unbroken' horse of his own. For thirty-three guineas.

For the rest of the next year, in addition to the milking, the ploughing and sowing, the harrowing and mowing, the contracting out to the County Council as a horse-and-cart 'man', and the stalking of every free-running rabbit in the countryside, Eddie trained that horse.

He 'broke it in'. Transformed it from nothing more than an attractive but unproductive, big strong animal, into a worthwhile piece of farmyard equipment. Trained it to pull a cart. And a whole variety of farm machinery.

Then he sold it. Twelve months later.

For sixty-six guineas!

And with his sixty-six guineas Eddie bought a number of henhouses. He realized that there was an opportunity for expansion in that line. The rearing of poultry was his next business venture. At fifteen coming sixteen...

It wasn't all work and no play for Eddie, however. Just, **nearly** all work and no play. There were some moments of light relief. Some high points of every year to which Eddie Stobart, as a growing boy, had always looked forward with eager anticipation. And one of these was the few weeks in every summer when he said 'Goodbye'to Bankdale Head. And went on holiday.

Not to the Canaries or the Carribean.

But to his cousins near Carlisle.

At Newhouse Farm.

4

MOLLY

—————————— ❖ ——————————

It was always great fun to go and stay at Newhouse Farm. With so
much company. Eddie had seven cousins living there. Two boys and
five girls.

As he was used to having just one litle brother, and plenty of hard
work, at home in Bankdale Head, company of his own age, and an absence
of work and responsibility for a week or two in the summer months was
a tremendous treat for Eddie. He always looked forward to it for months
beforehand.

As his two male cousins were both much older that he was, Eddie
spent most of his time, happily roaming around the farm, in the company
of the younger members of the family. Who were all girls.

When they were nine, and ten, and eleven, the girls loved to 'play
houses'. In an old hay-cart. Or in a not-yet-used or not-long-cleared corner
of a barn or hay-shed.

The location wasn't significant.

It was the improvisation that was the important, often almost the
inspired, thing.

Old wooden boxes doubled as tables and dressers. All shapes, and sizes, and colours of oddments of delph served as the crockery. And the 'ornaments'. Planks in varying thicknesses and degrees of woodworminess sufficed as 'sit-upons'. They were the chairs. Any old scrap of material, diligently 'pressed' became a 'curtain'. And old hessian sacks, disposed of because they had become so holey that they couldn't hold anything, were opened up, down the fraying cordy seams, to become the 'carpets'.

Since no proper house would be complete without the provision of something to eat, mud pie 'cakes' were the chief delicacy served with most of the 'meals'. These 'cakes' could differ greatly from 'baking' to 'baking', both in size and consistency. The size of the 'cake' depended upon the dimensions of the tin in which it was 'baked'. And that, in turn, depended upon whether it had contained Mansion floor polish or Cherry Blossom boot polish in its younger and more useful day. The consistency of the 'cake' depended on the gooeyness of its main ingredient. Mud. And the number of handfuls of grit and grass and gravel that had to be added to the 'mixture', to make it stick together, without sticking to the tin!

It was all magical make-believe!

The Johnston girls were thrilled to have cousin Eddie come to stay, too. It was wonderful what you could do, in a 'house', with a willing male. Not a big brother who laughed at you, and called you, 'stupid girls'.

Another reason why the girls were happy to have Eddie come to stay at Newhouse Farm 'on his holidays' was that he brought a bit of life and laughter, and a welcome variation into the daily routine of their lives. A sense of fun.

In the welcome cool, late on a summer evening, all the cousins really enjoyed sitting around, chatting and joking. It was when the sunlight of day yielded to the half-light of dusk that Eddie really came into his own. Telling the girls eerie, spooky ghost stories. He used to love to see them hunch their shoulders and pull their cardigans tightly round their little light summer dresses in mock terror. As darkness fell slowly and softly any sudden sound that shattered the silence, like the deep-throated lowing of a cow out on the pasture, or the sharp piercing bark of a hunting fox, became creepy.

And the more creepy it became, the more Eddie liked it. And the stories became more scary, too. To suit the surroundings!

Sometimes, as there were usually three of the girls playing 'house', the 'homemakers' split up. Two girls. And one girl, and one boy. Eddie.

This decision to expand their house-building skills was usually inspired by one of two reasons. Either an urge to compete and see who could make the better house, or a dispute over some trivial matter. This kind of 'fall-out' again occurred for one of two reasons. A disagreement about design, or a question of ownership. Where the table or the dresser should be placed in the 'living-room', or who actually 'owned', a scrap of crumpled cloth or a two-pound jampot.

When such divide-and-expand operations took place, Eddie always made sure, if he possibly could at all, that he was in Molly's house.

Eddie liked Molly. Not that he didn't like the rest, for he did.

They were all very kind to him. But Molly was different.

Just that little bit 'special'.

Molly appealed to Eddie particularly because she always made such a tidy house. And Eddie liked neat and tidy houses. He liked neat and tidy anythings. Molly had creative and different ideas about the way she used all the precious bits and pieces that were the furnishing and fittings for her house.

But there was more. There was something else. Something different and deeper about Molly that attracted Eddie to her. Something that was very real, but slightly more difficult to explain. It was the way that she seemed to understand him. Since she was nearly five years older than her cousin she was old enough to be a friend to him, to 'mother' him, and yet not 'boss him about'. And there was a genuine sense of peace about her whole personality, too.

Eddie liked being in Molly's house. It was a secure and satisfying, almost sanctified, place to be.

He always felt close to Molly.

As she grew older, it was inevitable that someone with Molly's looks, charm and personality would sooner or later attract the attention of the opposite sex. And she did. Molly had a boyfriend. Will Sarginson.

Like many girls in late teenage, Molly wanted to train for a job or profession, so she left the farm behind and went to commence nursing training in Manchester. Will, her boyfriend, missed her. And Eddie, her cousin, was always interested to hear of her progress. He was sure she would do well. She was bound to make such a wonderful nurse. So kind. And careful. And caring.

So much did Will miss her, indeed, that he set off for Manchester one weekend, with a singular purpose in view. He was going to propose to Molly Johnston. He wanted to marry her.

On arriving in Manchester, however, Will was distressed to discover that Molly was very ill. Dangerously ill. She had contracted a 'flu virus and medical staff were battling to save her life. But all in vain.

Molly, who had showed such promise in every aspect of life, died the next day. Aged nineteen.

What a blow to Will.

What a shock for the family.

What an emptiness for Eddie.

A few days later, young Eddie Stobart, then fifteen years of age, went along to the funeral. It was all so different from his memorable summer holidays at Newhouse Farm.

It was winter, for one thing. And the whole place was enveloped in an awesome gloom. The darkness of death. White-faced adults with red eyes tip-toed about. Nobody yelled or shouted or laughed in glee. There was nobody bent double in uncontrollable giggles, either.

Everybody spoke to anybody they decided to speak to at all, in subdued whispers.

As he approached the farmhouse door, Eddie saw Will Sarginson standing there, gazing blankly down the yard. Grieving. Alone with his thoughts. Dressed in black from head to toe, it seemed.

Eddie liked Will. He was a very sincere and friendly young man, some years older than he was. Since he didn't think that he would ever have been allowed to marry Molly himself, he wouldn't really have minded if Will had married her. They would have made a great couple, he had always been convinced. Will would have been kind to Molly, his friend, too, he was sure.

After a few sombre greetings, Will asked, "Would you like to come in and see Molly, Eddie?"

Young Eddie was taken aback for a moment.

"Yes. I think I might. I would, maybe," he replied at length, not terribly sure what to expect.

Although he wasn't sure of whether he wanted to 'see Molly' or not, he was too late to change his mind. He had said 'Yes', and to Will that meant that he did want to see her.

He had already pushed open the front door, and with the terse but tender invitation, "Come on," was already leading the way into the house.

Eddie followed. Reluctantly.

When they softly, silently, entered the darkened room where Molly lay motionless, Eddie was stunned. Startled, almost. To see the one that he had respected so much and laughed with so often, lying, still beautiful, marble-faced but so peaceful, in death.

Will stood on the other side of the coffin from his fifteen-year-old friend.

Looking across at Eddie, over the lifeless body of his beloved Molly, and bravely blinking back the tears, he said, gently, "Eddie, what you see there is only Molly's bodily remains. Her soul is with Jesus. She was prepared to die, Eddie. If it had been you, in this coffin, instead of her, would you have been prepared?"

This was challenge number two, to the teenage Eddie Stobart.

First his mother. Now Molly.

As he stood out in the yard, later, in those dragging-out minutes before the coffin was respectfully removed from the house, he looked idly around at the familiar farm buildings. Full of marvellous memories. The old hay cart lay lonely in a corner.

Molly wouldn't be making any more 'houses' there. She had gone to her eternal rest. Her 'long home'. 'A house not made with hands, eternal in the heavens'.

She had been prepared.

She had trusted in Christ as her Saviour when she just a little girl. She was ready to die. And ready for heaven.

She had been ready.

But what about Eddie?

While Eddie followed the funeral cortege as it wound its way slowly down the winter-bare lane, bearing Molly Johnston away from Newhouse Farm for the final time, he determined that he would have to get right with God.

'I will do that', he promised himself.

'Sometime. Soon, maybe.'

5

EDDIE READY

---❖---

When he had just turned seventeen years of age, Eddie learnt to drive. And he loved to drive, too. His father had replaced a succession of motor bikes with his first car, a Morris 8. Then, having developed a taste for the relative comfort of 'motoring', John Stobart traded in the 'Eight' for a brand new, shiny black, Morris 10, which he didn't seem all that keen to drive. Perhaps that was because he was never really given the chance!

Eddie loved that Morris 10. It was great to shine it up, and see it sparkle in the sun. But it was even better to get behind the wheel and get going. He became chauffeur to the family, when at all possible. Took them everywhere they wanted to go.

In November, 1946, one of the places that John Stobart, and his new wife, Ruth, liked to go to frequently was a Gospel mission in a Methodist chapel, fifteen miles from their home.

On most nights all four of them packed into the unheated Morris 10, wrapped up warmly for the journey, and set off for the mission. There were occasional nights when Ruth stayed at home with Ronnie, and Eddie and his father set out alone. No matter whoever else did, or didn't, go, though, Eddie went. He was the driver.

It was no hardship for him to go every night anyway. He wanted to go to the meetings. He thought that this was because the chapel was always comfortably heated, the singing was good, and the atmosphere welcoming. What he didn't understand immediately was that there was more to it than that. God was calling him. Speaking to him through the earnest addresses of the preacher, Herbert Silverwood.

A number of young men attended that mission every night. Some of them had just completed a course at Bible College, but Eddie suspected from some of the preacher's remarks the Mr. Silverwood fancied that all the preparation some of them had for Christian work was in their head. With nothing in their hearts. He kept warning his audience that a knowledge of the Bible, no matter how clever or academic, would not take anybody to heaven. They needed to trust in the Lord Jesus Christ, personally. Be saved by grace.

As he continued to hear the Gospel preached each night, Eddie came to realize that this was his opportunity. In these meetings, God by His Spirit was addressing the young man, directly. Confronting him with spiritual matters.

Was he now prepared to put his promise to himself, of two years before, into action. Was he going to trust Christ as his Saviour? Prepare to meet God, as Will had challenged?

This was his opportunity to begin a new life, in and for, Jesus, as his dying mother had so wished.

On Wednesday, 16th November, 1946, right in the middle of the middle week of the three-week mission, decision time came for Eddie. That evening, during the meeting in which Herbert Silverwood had again spoken of the sin of mankind, the love of God and the death of Christ to provide salvation from sin, Eddie determined that this was the night . He wasn't going to put it off any longer.

He knew that he needed to trust Christ.

He had known that since childhood. Since he had begun travelling about with his father, on the back of his motor bike. Hearing him preach the Gospel.

But now he wanted to trust in Christ. And that was different. He hadn't wanted to do that before. Now, he did.

At the close of the service, Herbert made his usual appeal. "Is there anyone in this church tonight who would like to commit their lives fully to the Lord Jesus Christ? He loves you, He came to earth to die for you, and now He is calling you to come to Him. If you would like to come to Jesus tonight, just make your way up to the front here so that we can see who you are, and we will be delighted to talk to you about the Saviour..."

There were two people who responded to that invitation to 'come up to the front', that night. One of them was the seventeen-year old Eddie Stobart. He had been waiting for that moment. He knew that an appeal would come at the end of the meeting. It always did. And he wanted to come to Christ.

As the congregation filed out into the winter night, Eddie was shown into a small room at the rear of the church building. There a lady spoke to him. Counselling him. She talked to him about the need to take 'the step of faith'. The importance of believing that Jesus had died for him, personally.

As the discussion continued, the patient counsellor compared this 'step of faith' to embarking upon a journey, by train. "You know, Eddie," she explained, "it is like a train waiting in a station. It is there to take you to your destination. Put you have to step on to it. You would never get anywhere, just standing on the platform."

Eddie smiled briefly. It was so basic. But so true. He hadn't time to dwell on the thought, however, for the lady beside him was in full flow... "And you don't need to worry about buying a ticket, either. Jesus paid the price for your salvation. All you have to do is trust Him. Step on board in faith, and He will do the rest. Keep you in this life, and take you safely, eventually, to His home in heaven."

It was there and then that Eddie recognised the simplicity of salvation. And there and then he bowed his head and simply accepted Christ as his Saviour. He took the step of faith.

From that moment on, Eddie was filled with a sense of security and satisfaction, and also with a sense of ambition and direction.

The sense of security and satisfaction came from knowing that he was ready to meet God. Will's challenge at Molly's funeral had never left him. 'Are you prepared?' he had enquired, pointedly.

The answer to that question then, had been, 'No'. He wasn't ready.

The answer to that same question, now, however, was 'Yes'. Eddie was now prepared for life. And for death.

Eddie was ready.

But there was more to his salvation, than just preparing to meet God in a future day, and for a life in heaven, although those things were true. And important. Becoming a Christian had also give him an ambition in relation to his life on earth. A purpose and direction for living.

From that November night, Eddie determined that he was going to fulfil his mother's dying wish. He had now trusted in Jesus. Now he was going to 'grow up to love Him'. And live for Him. Every day, and in every circumstance, of his life.

Eddie was now ready.

For anything.

For God.

6

MY KIND OF GIRL

❖

After his conversion, and with a mind at peace with itself, Eddie began to direct his thoughts to other matters. Lighter concerns. Affairs of the heart.

Since he had now reached late teenage and didn't have many close companions of his own age, Eddie decided that he would like, sometime, and sooner rather than later, to meet somebody whose company he would really enjoy. Someone to talk to. To share with. It would be an added bonus, too, if that person should just turn out to be female!

He would see. God, in time, would probably show him the right person. The person that he had prayed he would meet. The person he had imagined he would like to meet. For Eddie had, in his head, a list of qualities, a kind of check-list of virtues, that this friend-to-be of his should possess.

She would be pleasant, hardworking, understanding, tidy... These qualities would be desirable. But variable. No hard and fast rules about them.

There was one feature about his kind of girl that would be absolutely vital, though.She would have to be a Christian. Have the same nature as him. The new nature. After all, if she wasn't, what would they get to talk about? Or have in common?

They wouldn't share the same goal in life, either.

For Eddie wanted to live for Jesus.

Then one day it seemed that his dream was beginning to come true. He overheard a conversation about a girl called Nora Boyd. This person lived near him, it seemed. In the village of Caldbeck, just over two miles from Hesket Newmarket. And the point of the whole story, to which Eddie rapidly became an eager eavesdropper, was that this Nora Boyd, whoever she was, had just recently 'got saved'.

Eddie's heart skipped a beat or two. Could this be the kind of girl that he wanted to meet? Sometime. If she was saved she fulfilled the most essential of his unwritten essential criteria. She was a Christian. But what was she like? And what age was she, anyway?

He would have to find out more.

So for the next few days Eddie made a number of discreet but diligent enquiries. And made a number of pleasing and interesting discoveries.

Nora Boyd, he learnt from 'usually reliable sources', was an attractive young lady, of around his own age. She lived in Caldbeck, it was true, but the bad news was that she worked, and stayed, away from home, most of the time. She was employed as a housekeeper to a family in Lockerbie, Scotland. The good news, however, was that she returned to her Cumbrian village home on her weekend off, once a month.

Having obtained her Lockerbie address, Eddie wrote to Nora. And he spent some time over the composition of his letter too. It was vital that his wording expressed his thinking, accurately. It had to be right. Spot on. Sincere but not solemn. Friendly but not sloppy...

The purpose of his letter was threefold. Initially, he wrote to encourage the new Christian by telling her that he had heard of her conversion. Then he introduced himself, telling Nora that he also had been saved just recently.

The first half of the letter was all about the blessings of faith in Christ and the privilege and responsibility of living for Him.

The letter concluded with what was, basically, the whole point of the exercise. The tentative suggestion that perhaps they 'could meet sometime'.

Then he waited anxiously for a reply.

Would she receive his letter? Would she reply to it?

Would she even consider him worth bothering about? Or would she think him bold? Or just plain stupid?

All kinds of weird thoughts rumbled and rattled around in his mind, like the wee stones that rumbled and rattled around in the big hollow roller as his team of horses had pulled it up and down the fields in the springtime. Years ago.

About a week after he had written his letter, Eddie had the first of his questions answered. He was absolutely delighted to receive a reply.

It was also very pleasing to discover, after he had carefully, almost tenderly, opened the envelope, that Nora's reply was written in much the same vein as his initial letter. She thanked him for his letter. Was pleased to find out that he was a Christian. And encouraged him in his walk for God.

The exciting bit of that reply, for the expectant Eddie came in the last paragraph. Yes. Nora would like to meet him sometime. And even went so far as to suggest that they begin attending the Saturday night Bible Rallies in Hebron Hall, a Brethren assembly, in Carlisle, together. It would be an ideal place to go, for they would meet other Christians, of around their own age, there.

Eddie was thrilled.

Not only had Nora's reply been so positive, but her suggestion of where they could go was excellent. It really appealed to him, the whole set-up.

However, now that Nora had agreed to go to the Bible Rallies in Carlisle with Eddie, the next question in the young man's mind was, 'How will we get on?' What would this Nora be like, as a person? He had no doubt whatsoever that she was a sincere Christian. But would she possess any of his other desirable characteristics? This thought crossed his mind but didn't remain there. To worry him. For he was convinced that God had overruled in the whole matter to date, and He didn't make any mistakes.

On the Saturday of their first 'date', in early December, 1946, Eddie spent a good part of the day shining up. First he shined up his father's Morris 10, for he was determined to pick up his new friend in style. Then he spent the remainder of the time shining up himself ! It would be important to impress. Right from the start.

The first night went well.

Eddie liked this Nora from the moment they met.

For in addition to being a genuine Christian, she seemed to be kind and understanding. Pleasant in personality. Particular about her appearance. He couldn't be quite sure yet if she was hardworking or not, but he would find out about that in due course, no doubt !

They had so much in common. So much to talk about.

Eddie had Nora had both come from interesting backgrounds. They were able to share that together.

Eddie and Nora had both come to know Christ as Saviour within two months of each other. They really enjoyed sharing that together, too. And how also, they both wanted to be as effective as possible in their Christian lives. This was by far the most important, the most vital, point of contact between the two teenagers.

Then there was their work. Which was so different. Eddie talked to Nora about hen houses and threshing mills. She in turn was able to inform him on the finer points concerning such household matters as cooking and cleaning, washing and ironing. After listening to her chattering away about her work, and her workplace, for a while, Eddie concluded that she had all the right experience in all the right kind of skills! And she was probably hardworking, too. The kind of young lady that kept things moving about a place. He liked that.

Since their first night had been such a success, they agreed to start attending the Bible Rally in Hebron Hall, every Saturday night when Nora was at home. For as well as him liking her, she appeared to be impressed with the unaffected and unpretentious Eddie, too. She even proved willing to use some of her meagre pay to demonstrate that in a practical way.

It was on their last outing before their first Christmas together, that she did so. Somewhat shyly she produced a tastefully wrapped present for him. And it displayed her ability to make sensible decisions at an early age. Her pick of a present for her new friend, Eddie, was an ideal choice for a young man embarking upon the Christian life.

It was an illustrated copy of John Bunyan's book, 'Pilgrim's Progress'.

7

GOD LOVES YOU, CHILD

❖

I n those happy, early, dates-with-Eddie days, Nora Boyd often reflected
upon the goodness and wisdom of God. How He had overruled in
her life, up until that point...

She had never known her father, and so when her mother died
when she was only four years old, Nora was left an orphan at that early
age. After some time was spent being shuttled between two Children's
Homes, Nora and her brother were eventually settled in a suitable and
caring foster home in Caldbeck, Cumberland. Next village to Hesket
Newmarket, where Eddie lived.

During her childhood years in Caldbeck, Nora was sent along to
school, and to Sunday School, but she knew, and heard, little of the Gospel.
She didn't realize that there was a God of love, who cared for someone
like her. And Who wanted her to be his child, by faith.

A foster-child, in the 1930's was expected to become self-
supporting, as soon as possible, so Nora left school at fourteen years of
age, and started work as a trainee live-in houskeeper in the home in
Lockerbie.

In September, 1946, when she was seventeen, relatives of her foster-parents invited her to stay with them for a week's holiday, at their home in Liverpool. Nora was thrilled at the thought of a week in the city of Liverpool, but she had only one reservation about it. She had a good friend called Annie Teasdale, and they went about everywhere together. Nora wouldn't really like to go without Annie. Could she possibly come along as well, she wondered?

No problem, came the reply from Liverpool. Certainly. Bring Annie. She would be welcome, too.

What Nora and Annie didn't fully realize, however, was that their kind holiday hosts were also sincere Christians. And they longed to see others brought to faith in Christ.

On the Saturday of their stay, 'Uncle Billy', as Nora had often been instructed with a smile, to call him, asked the two girls if they would like to go along to a meeting in a boxing stadium, that evening. It was to be a single, well-publicized, follow-up rally to an earlier mission by a big man called Stan Ford, who had been a boxer himself, before his conversion. Nora and her friend liked the idea. As long as it was going to be preaching, and not boxing, in the stadium. They didn't fancy watching two men thumping each other silly, and since they had never been to anything like a boxing arena before, they recognised that their only opportunity to be in one would probably be that night. They certainly would never be at a boxing match!

When they went along, with 'Uncle Billy', later that day, the two teenage girls discovered that the stadium was filling fast. Many people had come, like themselves, obviously out of curiosity to savour the atmosphere of a vast arena. Used for a totally unusual purpose.

On all four sides of the stadium, tiers of cinema-type pull-down-bang-up seats looked down upon the central item. The focal point. The boxing ring.

The service began with the singing of some Gospel hymns. These were unfamiliar to Nora. She had never heard most of them before. And it must have been something different, too, for that stadium, to resound to the strains of enthusiastic hymn-singing rather than the fanatical cheering of boxing fans.

When Stan Ford climbed through the ropes, into his 'pulpit', the ring, Nora was impressed with the sheer physical size of the man. He was big, and strong. With huge hands. But when he opened his Bible and began to read from it, she discovered that his nature contrasted sharply with his outward appearance. He was soft and sincere. Caring and gentle. Like somebody who had something which he considered important, to put across to his audience. Something which they should definitely know about.

As he began to addresss his large and attentive congregation, the speaker had a problem. Since the arena was a square, and he was standing right in the centre of it, he always had his back to somebody. He surmounted this difficulty by keeping constantly on the move whilst speaking, turning continually to maintain contact with all sections of his audience.

The fact that he had a strong and resonant voice helped, too. For even though Nora and Annie couldn't always see his face they could always hear his message!

And what he said struck a chord in the heart of Nora Boyd.

Stan Ford was talking about love. And especially the love of God.

As a child, Nora hadn't known a great deal about parental love. As an orphan, she was placed in a foster-home where she was shown kindness and consideration and that was the best that she could ever have hoped for. Indeed, as she had grown older she had recognized that as a blessing. Many others, who had been in her kind of situation had fared rather worse.

She had never experienced the warmth and depth of family love, however.

There had been times when she felt looked after, but unloved.

Now, here was a man, standing in the middle of a boxing ring, in the middle of Liverpool, reading from the Bible about the love of God. And actually saying that God loved **her**! What was more, he said that God loved her so very much that He gave His only Son, Jesus, to die on a cross to take away her sins. And if she responded to that love, if she believed that Jesus had died for her, and accepted Him into her heart and life, then she would become His child. She would be adopted into the family of God. For ever.

Nora was absolutely overwhelmed!

She had never heard the like of this before!

God loved her. Christ had died for her. And she could become a child of God by simply trusting in Jesus.

As the meeting drew towards its close, Nora came to Christ. Quietly, sincerely, in her own heart, she said, "Thank you, God, for loving me. I want to be a child in your family. I know Jesus died for me. Please accept me as one of your children, now."

Before he finished speaking, Stan Ford invited anyone who was interested 'in coming to Christ for salvation' to wait behind afterwards and speak to him, or some of the other Christians. And he also advised anybody who had trusted in the Saviour during the meeting to tell someone. 'Confess with your mouth the Lord Jesus.'

But Nora, the new convert, did neither.

Although she was extremely happy, her feelings an inexplicable blend of peace and excitement, she didn't tell anybody. Yet. She was scared to. It all seemed so wonderful. So unreal, somehow. Perhaps it would all have gone, evaporated, disappeared, by the morning.

She would wait.

So she just went back to 'Uncle Billy's' house with the rest of the family. And Annie.

Next day was Sunday, and on Sundays 'Uncle Billy' taught the Bible Class in the local church Sunday School. He invited his two guests to come along with him, and Nora who would once have been rather cautious of 'things religious', was only too happy to accept his invitation.

There was this strange kind of new kind of feeling inside her now. It seemed to have kindled a desire to find out more and more about the love of God which she had heard about for the very first time, and that had so arrested her, the night before. And she wanted to learn more about living for her Lord.

What did she do now? Where did she go from here? What next?

There were so many questions. And she needed so many answers.

At the Bible Class, Billy was telling all the others of 'the great meeting', on the previous night. Recounting, at least in part, the main thrust of the message.

As he spoke of the love of God, and the death of the Lord Jesus, and how He was still calling others to 'come unto Him', some of the Bible Class members told of how, and when, they had come to faith in Christ.

Nora saw her opportunity. And almost impulsively, she seized it.

"I was saved in the meeting in the boxing arena last night," she stated simply.

Everyone appeared pleased that this girl whom most of them didn't even know, had come to Liverpool, and to the Lord, all in the same week.

Although all the others smiled reassuringly, and appeared pleased, 'Uncle Billy' make no effort whatsoever to disguise his absolute delight. He wasn't long home that afternoon until everybody in the house knew of Nora's conversion! There could be no hiding it now!

At the end of their week's holiday, both Nora and Annie had to return home rather reluctantly. And Nora had to go back to her work, in Lockerbie.

Now, though, she was a different person. Something marvellous had happened in her life. She wanted to go to church. And she would dearly love to meet some other Christians.

Inspired by such desires, on the Sunday evening just eight days after coming to know Christ as her Saviour, Nora Boyd set out to walk the streets of Lockerbie. She was looking for a church to go to. And Christians, like herself, to talk to.

As she approached a small and plain-looking building Nora saw that there was a man standing on the pavement outside it. He seemed to be handing out bits of paper to the people who were passing. He was saying something to the most of them, too.

When the new Christian teenager reached him, he offered her one of his bits of paper. "Would you take a tract?" he enquired, graciously. That must be what the bits of paper are called, Nora surmised. Tracts.

"Yes, thank you," Nora replied, taking the 'tract'. And glad of the contact.

"Would you like to come into our meeting?" the gentleman continued. "You will be very welcome."

Could this be the answer to Nora's need for Christian company?

"Yes, I wouldn't mind," she responded at once, trying to appear as matter-of-fact as possible. She liked the man. And it would be wonderful to feel 'very welcome'.

As she entered the unembellished building, escorted by the man who had invited her in, Nora noticed the name of the 'church'.

It was Lockerbie Gospel Hall.

When she had been duly furnished with a hymn-book, the man-with-the-tracts showed Nora into a seat beside his wife. Then he also later came and sat with them.

Nora felt at ease with that couple, almost at once. An immediate but invisible bond developed between them, there and then.

As they were parting after the service, to allow Nora to return to the house where she worked, they invited her to come back on the following Sunday. Nora did that happily. Indeed she looked forward to it all week. Then, on that second Sunday she was invited to return on the following week, with an exciting extension. She was asked to come to the home of her newly-found friends, Mr. and Mrs. James, and join them for supper after the service.

This was something new for the usually housebound housekeeper. But it presented her with a problem, as well.

She would have to ask for time off her work, if she was to accept this very kind invitation. And that she did. During the week she approached her employers, asking for a few extra hours off on the following Sunday evening. In order to attend 'church' with some friends and then spend some time with them afterwards.

Nora was soon to discover a principle that she was set to prove true repeatedly in later life. When God wanted her to do something, He was always three or four steps ahead of her in the planning of it.

Her employers agreed readily to her having a Sunday afternoon off, on a regular basis, and they went even farther than that. Since she had worked so well for so long, they suggested allowing her to have another afternoon per week off, also.

Nora appreciated this, and opted for a Wednesday.

During the next few months, in that little Scottish town, Mr. and Mrs. James, and their niece and her husband, Mary and Alex. Traille, did everything they possibly could to help the new Christian in their area, Nora Boyd, who had become a regular attender at the Sunday evening meetings in their assembly, and a regular visitor in their home on her Wednesday afternoon off. She had a heartful of love for the Saviour and a headful of questions about the Christian faith.

Here were people with whom Nora easily identified. They answered all her questions about the Bible, which she had begun to read every day, and practical Christian living, and showed her unlimited hospitality. Lovingly and patiently they nurtured her in her newly-found faith.

It was at tea in the James home too, one Sunday evening after a meeting, that Nora met the man who had been the speaker for that evening,

Jim Hyslop. This man, it seemed, preached in many of the assemblies in the north of England, and in southern Scotland. During the round-the-table discussion that evening Nora heard her friends discuss the well-attended especially-geared-towards-young-believers rallies which were held on alternate Saturday evenings in Hebron Hall, Carlisle. She gathered, also, that a number of the young Christians from the Lockerbie area attended those meetings. And seemed to be helped and encouraged by them.

This information was to prove particularly useful when framing her reply to a letter which she was soon to receive from a recently-converted farming lad from Hesket Newmarket. Eddie Stobart.

8

ALWAYS LEAVE THE
STACKYARD TIDY

❖

In October, 1946, before Eddie knew either the Lord, or Nora, something happened that was to launch him out on a business venture. On his own.

A man came to Bankdale Head Farm to do the threshing. In the days before combine-harvesters, contractors travelled around amongst the farming community, hiring out their services. Threshing corn. This was one such man.

In the course of the day's work, the threshing-machine owner happened to remark to Eddie that he was contemplating giving up the threshing business. Packing it in. And selling it out.

"I am totally fed up with this whole carry-on now," he explained later, over a cup of tea. "It is too tiring, and too constant work. Trailing about all over the country."

" If I could only find somebody to buy all this stuff," he went on, waving his hand out towards the spot in the stackyard where the thresher was rumbling and rattling away, driven by a broad belt from a stationary tractor, "I would be out of it tomorrow".

This declaration immediately set the mind of the seventeen-year-old Eddie awhirl. He reckoned that this would be a great job for him. But where on earth would he find enough money to buy a threshing machine? And a tractor?

Later on that evening Eddie was milking the cows when his father came into the byre. As they chatted through the day's events he told his father of the threshing-man's disillusionment, and his desire to sell up and get out. He also told him of his dream. Buying over the whole outfit.

John Stobart realized that this was an ideal opportunity for his go-ahead son to branch out on another enterprise. Extend his working options. He reached for the bucket of warm, frothy milk which Eddie held out to him, exchanging it for an empty one. Then, as more milk tinkled into the bottom of an enamel bucket, he made a proposal.

He offered to buy Eddie's henhouses, with their resident poultry, for as much as it would take for him to purchase all the threshing machinery.

Eddie was pleased with this suggestion. It was a reasonable, and considerate plan. So he went next day to see the threshing-mill man. After some discussion of prices, Eddie agreed to buy all the anxious-to-retire man's gear. A Ransomes threshing machine. A Case tractor to tow it and drive it. Various other belts and tools. And the 'goodwill' of the business. The names and addresses of over two hundred regular customers...

Eddie was all set up to set out on his own.

Or so he thought.

During the summer months, in addition to working at home at Bankdale Head, Eddie had been working under contract to a number of local farmers. And the local Council. For this he used the home-farm Ferguson tractor with a whole host of accessory implements.

Eddie worked hard at every job he could possibly find, with that tractor. For there were real needs back at home. His father and stepmother had started to have a family and by that time there were four extra little mouths to feed. Jim, Alan, Mary and Ruth were Eddie's half-brothers and sisters, and he wanted to do everything he possibly could to help in the raising of them.

Now he had his own equipment, he could attract more business. Bring in more money, for the family and himself. It would be great for all of them.

Or so he thought.

Although most of the harvesting of the crop took place in autumn, the threshers were kept busy from August until the April of the following year. Corn was overwintered in large stacks in the farmyard, and only threshed when the farmers needed either straw for bedding, or grain for feeding. And the seed grain for sowing in the next spring wasn't threshed until it was needed. In the next spring. On many small farms storage space was at a premium, and it was simpler, and cheaper, to keep the unthreshed corn in the stackyard.

This method of storing the corn over the winter was also greatly appreciated by the multitudes of rats and mice who made their homes at the heart of the stacks. After all what could be better during during the freezing, starving, windy winter months?

Warmth, food, and shelter. All for free!

In those early taking-over-the-business months, however, those months when he came to know both the Lord, and Nora, things didn't take off just as Eddie had expected. Of the over two hundred 'regular' customers he was expecting, less than one hundred hired Eddie and his recently-acquired machinery, to do their work.

This was a blow. A big disappointment.

When he enquired into it, Eddie discovered that there were, apparently, two reasons for this. By far the more common of the two was that he was 'far too young'. 'What would a seventeen year old lad know about threshing, never mind about doing a full day's work?' hard-headed farmers argued. Threshing was 'man's work'. And the fact that the chap whom Eddie had engaged as his assistant was only sixteen, didn't help much either!

A couple of youngsters with a threshing mill. 'No way we will be risking them on our farms,' they said.

The not so prevalent, but much-more-hurtful-to-Eddie reason, given for not employing him to thresh their corn, was that he was a 'Methodist'. It wasn't long until young Eddie discovered that many of those who made this excuse had no problems with the Methodist Church. What they really meant, their real reason, for not employing the seventeen-year-old, who was starting out on his own, was that he was a Christian.

Even as a mere babe in the faith Eddie was being asked to pay the price for identification with Christ.

It was annoying. Frustrating. Sickening, almost.
Cost him worried days. And sleepless nights.
What could he do about it, though? How did he tackle this problem? Overcome this obstacle? Had he made a big mistake in thinking that he could 'make it' as a threshing contractor?

During the summer of 1947, when he had just turned eighteen, Eddie, the young Christian, was invited to give his testimony, tell of his faith in Christ, in the Mission Hall in Blennerhasset, about fifteen miles from his home.

After the service, Eddie was invited out to the home of Mr. and Mrs. John Millican for supper. It was a lovely summer evening, and as they waited for the supper to be served, Eddie and the much older John sat in the greenhouse, chatting. They were making the best of the last of the heat of what had been a fine July day.

When John enquired, almost casually, "Well, how did you get on at the threshing last season, Eddie?" the once hopeful but by then somewhat depressed young guest opened up his heart.

"I was a bit disappointed in it, to tell you the truth," he confided. Then proceeded to elaborate. He was glad of someone like John to talk to. So he just told the obviously interested and well experienced Christian of all his concerns. And the pathetic-to-him reasons that had been advanced for not using his services.

When Eddie had explained his perplexing plight at length, John had one or two pertinent questions to ask. Then, when he was sure that he understood the picture perfectly, John Millican did two things.

He gave him some good advice.

And he commited the whole situation to God in prayer, encouraging Eddie to do the same.

The advice with which he commenced was sound. And practical.

"Find out how the job should be done properly, Eddie, and always do it that way. To the best of your ability. Every time," he advocated. "What you need to do is to build up a reputation for doing a good job, in the countryside. Always remember the old saying that you are 'only as good as your last job'.

And attend carefully to the maintenance of you equipment. That is important, too."

Looking over at the attentive, aspiring-thresher-operator, after he had delivered those gems of practical wisdom, John said, "I think we should pray about this, Eddie."

So they did. Both of them.

John first. Then Eddie.

A strange sense of the presence of God pervaded that greenhouse, with its moist heat and musky scent of tomato plants, as the two men rolled the entire threshing matter over into the omnipotent hands of their Heavenly Father.

When they had finished praying, John must have known, or perhaps he merely hoped, that the supper was nearly ready, for he summed up the discussion with words of reassurance.

"Well that's it. Don't worry any more about it, Eddie. Just have faith in God. He will honour you," he counselled.

Then, rising to go back into the house, for the supper which was indeed ready, John Millican made his absolutely-final, final comment, adding, "Oh, and by the way, there is something I forgot to tell you earlier. Always leave the stackyard tidy."

When the next threshing season began, in August, Eddie remembered, and took, John's advice. He always made sure that his equipment was in perfect working order, and he did his utmost to ensure that the corn was being threshed properly. This meant constantly checking the quality and quantity of the 'pickle' coming through. And making sure that none of it ended up in the chaff!

He kept himself ever watchful. Endlessly monitoring.

It wasn't difficult for the neat-by-nature Eddie to 'always leave the stackyard tidy', either. That was one of the things he had been trying to do from the very start. He paid extra and particular attention to it now, though.

And the God to whom John and Eddie had committed the whole affair, that summer night, did as John had predicted. He honoured the young man's dedication. And diligence.

Throughout the autumn and winter months, the phone at Bankdale Head kept ringing.

"Eddie, I know I haven't used you before, but I am out of straw and I would like you to thresh a stack for me," a caller would request.

Or, "I have only about a week's feeding left for my animals Eddie, and I need a wee bit of threshing done. I was talking to old Frank

Farmerson the other day and he told me that he was very pleased with your work. Could you come over some of these days and do a stack for me?" some potential new customer would enquire.

Eddie had acquired, with the help of God and through patience, persistence, and dogged determination, what John had said he needed. A reputation amongst the farming community for 'doing a good job'.

Over the next two seasons, Eddie had all the work he could contend with. And more.

At the end of the second year, Eddie's father bought another threshing mill, to help cope with the demand. And at the end of the third season they were forced to buy a third machine between them.

When Ronnie left school at sixteen, he helped in the threshing business, too. And there was enough work to keep three machines, Eddie, his father and brother, and four additional men all busy.

As the business began to flourish Eddie tried to instil into all those working with and around him the principles that John Millican had taught him that evening in the greenhouse.

They always did the best job possible.

They always left the stackyard tidy.

And that policy was to prove productive. In a number of unexpected ways.

One of Eddie's regular and best customers in those early hiring-out-his own threshing mill days was Mr. George Scott, who was a very big man. Tall and hefty. Physically powerful.

What surprised Eddie about George Scott from the very first day when he trailed his thresher onto his farm was that the man never seemed to do a single thing himself. Whether he was so overweight that he couldn't, or so overbearing that he never needed to, the young threshing contractor could never quite figure out. All that he discovered was that George Scott had become an expert in giving orders. And such was his reputation that every farmhand within a ten mile radius seemed to dance attendance on him!

However, this fearsome farmer offered Eddie Stobart guaranteed work. He was to thresh corn on Mr. Scott's farm every other Monday and Tuesday. This should have been very satisfying to Eddie. But it wasn't. Really. He found it extremely frightening. He was dead scared of the giant of a man who used to poke him in the ribs with his stick and curse and bawl at him.

"Hurry up young Stobart! Surely you can put more through than this!" he would shout above the din of the machinery, or, "Just look at those tyings. That will never do!"

And Eddie was trying ever so hard. To do the best job possible.

So there was one Sunday night every fortnight when Eddie Stobart didn't sleep. Not a wink. Hardly ever closed an eye. Contemplating Monday morning to come...

At the end of his first year contracting to George Scott, the man with the powerful presence and ever-poking-stick called Eddie aside.

"I want to talk to you about next year, young man," he began, gruffly.

Great, thought Eddie. He has given me such a hammering, he can't be happy. This is one contract that I don't really care if I have renewed or not. If somebody else gets his business next year, I will get a lot more sleep!

"What about next year?" Eddie asked, innocently. It would be rather imprudent to go public with his innermost thoughts.

"I am going to pay you an extra pound for your year's work," George Scott went on. "And for as long as I live I want you to do my threshing. I have tried my best to scare the wits out of you since you came to work for me, and I have failed. And noboby, I mean **nobody**, could have done a better job for me than you have!"

Eddie's face glowed with pride and his heart thumped off the soles of his boots all at once.

"Fine, Mr. Scott, fine! Thank you. Thank you!" he replied with a genial grin, not daring to ask the immediate question that sprang into his mind. It was, "How long are you going to live for, then?"!

Things settled down, though.

Eddie gradually became accepted, then respected, by George Scott.

This was to be proved by something which happened a few years later.

It was a pleasant autumn day on the Scott farm. Trees and hedgerows changing colour. Hips and haws glinting red in the sunshine-with-a-nip. Eddie and his team working away, in top gear.

Then the big man himself came lumbering across the stackyard. He made a kind of a waving, beckoning gesture with the dreaded stick which he always carried.

"Eddie, will you come over here and talk to me a while?" he invited.

Knowing the man a lot better, Eddie wasn't just quite so scared now. He was ever respectful, though. Could well do without any more bruised ribs.

When Eddie approached the man who had employed him to do his threshing for a number of seasons, George Scott said, "Sit down here on a bale beside me, Eddie. I want to ask you something."

Eddie complied. Sat down on the twenty per cent of the indicated bale that was not occupied by the considerable physical frame of George Scott.

As they sat relaxing, watching the men working away, and listening to the machinery droning monotonously on, the outsize farmer put his question.

"Eddie, could you tell me how to get to heaven?" was his simple, if somewhat startling, request.

Then he went on to explain.

"You see, Eddie, you have no idea what a bad man George Scott has been. On my last farm in west Cumberland I used to go to the market, and sell potatoes. Then I drank the money. Every penny of it. I hardly ever gave my wife enough to keep us on. That poor woman has had a miserable life with me..." And so it went on. Until the man who had so terrorised the young Eddie Stobart had poured out his whole stricken heart to him.

When, at last, George had concluded his string of confessions with the plaintive plea, "Eddie, what can I do?", the Christian contractor gave him his answer.

"We don't get to heaven by doing anything, Mr Scott. It is not our good deeds that take us there," he explained. "We get to heaven through faith in what Christ has done for us on the cross two thousand years ago. In this matter there are no big sinners, and no small sinners. We have all sinned. But on the cross Jesus died to take away our sins. And He will do that if we come to Him, believing that He died for us. And if we trust in Him as our Saviour, then we will get to heaven."

George Scott listened intently to all that Eddie had to say.

Then he rose slowly, leaning heavily on his stick.

"Thanks, Edddie, " he said before turning away.

As he sat motionless on his end of the bale, watching the bulky farmer shuffling back towards the farmhouse, Eddie was glad that he had persisted with George Scott. Through all the daunting, difficult days.

For he had always done the best job possible for him.

Had always left his stackyard tidy.

And had been afforded the opportunity of telling him, at his own request, how he could 'get to heaven'.

9

A GOOD IDEA

❖

During the early days of their courtship, Nora and Eddie only saw each other very occasionally. Usually on Nora's weekends off from her work in Lockerbie.

She was busy. He was busy. And they were thirty miles apart.

Then, during the summer of 1947, Nora moved south to Carlisle to work. She moved in with, and worked for, the Proudfoot family in the city.

This proved to be a beneficial move to her for a number of reasons. For one, the pay was better, and for two she was able to see Eddie a lot more often. He was only fourteen miles away now, and she had more time off. This pleased them both. A lot.

In those years at Carlisle, too, Nora progressed spiritually as she gradually became involved in the work and worship at Hebron Hall. In addition to going along to all the Saturday night rallies with Eddie and their friends Richard Jardine and Betty Murray, she became a regular attender at the Sunday services. As often as her household duties permitted.

Nora soon began to participate in the work of that assembly. She was baptised and became a member of the church. And she was also pleased to be asked to use her obvious-to-others and varied, unfolding talents, in another way. She became a Sunday School teacher.

For the next few years, when Eddie was working long hours with his threshing machines, and Nora was working in Carlisle, they saw each other as often as they could.

The friendship was becoming a relationship.

Liking was maturing into love.

Then a further move for Nora made meeting up much easier again. She returned to Caldbeck, her home village, to work for the local doctor and his wife. Helping with the housework. Caring for the children. A 'nanny', really.

Since Hesket Newmarket and Caldbeck were neighbouring villages, the two busy young people, both keen Christians, began to meet more often. They spent a few holidays together, too, with Richard and Betty.

In July 1951, however, something simple happened which was to change the situation for all of them. Totally unexpectedly, Eddie received a letter from his uncle Wilfred. It was to say that the tenants who had lived in a house he had to rent, were leaving, and he was offering it to Eddie, before letting anyone else know of the vacancy.

Very kind of uncle Wilfred. Very good of him to think of his hard-working nephew. And it would probably be a good idea for him to move out, for Bankdale Head had started to become just that little bit crowded. Jim, Alan, Mary and Ruth were all developing physically. Rapidly. Eating more. And requiring more space. So what with the family of father, mother and four growing children, plus Ronnie and himself, space was at a premium.

A move out to a house of his own would give him more room. And greater independence. But what would he do on his own in a house of his own? The farm contractor knew plenty about ploughing and threshing, but precious little about cooking and cleaning, washing and ironing. He had always been used to having someone behind, at home, to do that kind of thing for him.

So he saw this as his opportunity. The chance of a house to let, in a district and at a time when houses to let were almost non-existent, accelerated his actions on something he had been contemplating for quite a while. He liked Nora. Loved her, he would admit, secretly. She had fulfilled, unknown to herself, all his unwritten want-list of personal attributes. And her vibrant and rapidly-developing Christian faith attracted him to her, more and more, every time they met.

He was sure he would like to marry her. Spend the rest of his life with her.

But did she feel the same way about him? He knew that the only means he could employ to be certain of the answer to that question was the direct one.

He would have to ask it.

To her.

As Nora had the next afteroon off, she had promised to travel across to Bankdale Head, to see Eddie. And he decided that he would wait until then to put his question.

He did. But it proved difficult. There were so many things to think about. So many plans to make if she said 'Yes'. The possibility of her saying 'No' was not an option that he had time to dwell long upon.

It was a pleasant summer aftrernoon when the young man with the big question in his heart spied his girlfriend coming up the lane. And he couldn't even wait until she reached the door. Anyway, there were too many little ones around, for such important matters to be approached in the house.

So, walking out, he met her in the lane.

He had a well-read letter in his pocket. And an oft-rehearsed question on his lips.

Eddie was more pragmatic, than romantic, though.

With him, if a thing had to be said or done, it had to be said or done. Forget about the frills. Forgo the fancies.

As soon as they had met, then, and after they had exchanged remarks about 'the nice day', Eddie said, "I had a letter yesterday from my uncle Wilfred".

"Oh," replied Nora, wondering what this was about or before. "And what was he saying or wanting?"

"It was just to tell me that he has a house to let, and I ...or I mean we, can have it if we want it. I was just wondering if we should get married and live in it."

Eddie stopped in the lane. He had said his bit. Made his proposal. As best he could. All that remained for him to do now was wait for the answer. And he wasn't going another inch until he heard it!

Nora had gone a step or two ahead. She, too, stopped. Then turned to look at him.

This was all so sudden. Deep in the heart of her she had been wondering when, if ever he was going to ask her to marry him. But she had this romantic image of her-husband-to-be, down on one knee, in a firelit, candlelit room, with a bunch of red roses. Not of the two of them standing in the middle of a country lane on a sunny-but-breezy day, flanked by the last of the season's cow-parsley!

But that was just typical Eddie. Practical as ever. And she loved him. And he had asked her. So she had to answer him. He was standing there. Waiting.

After what seemed an age to Eddie, she gave her reply, smiling.

"Yes," she said, trying hard to conceal her absolute delight, and trying to be as matter-of-fact as he was, "that would probably be a good idea."

So that was it.

Eddie had popped his question.

Nora had given her answer. 'A good idea.' He thought so too.

They were engaged to be married now, and there was no sense in hanging about. They might as well arrange for it as soon as possible.

For their house was soon to become vacant!

When Eddie took over tenancy of what was to be the first-home-together for his wife-to-be Nora, and himself , at Quarry House, Brocklebank, in October, 1951, it was a cold, empty, echoing shell. They would need furniture, some at least, to start off with. But where did you go to find it? Enough to furnish a house?

It wasn't long until he had the answer. Now that Nora had given him a positive, 'good-idea' response to his primary question, he would find the answer to any others that cropped up. They could only be minor in comparison. Surely.

An elderly uncle had left Eddie one hundred pounds in his will. To be paid after he turned twenty-one years of age. And Eddie was now twenty-two.

He would use that money to furnish their new home, he decided. But when on earth would he and Nora ever find time off together to go and browse around showrooms? She was very busy in the doctor's house. And it was autumn. His busiest time of the year with the thresher.

The only possible solution to either of them finding time to go looking for a houseful of furniture came later in the month.

It was a wet day. A pouring wet and windy day. And Eddie wouldn't be going out with the machines. So he took the day off and went shopping.

Someone had told him of a good saleroom in Carlisle. They had, apparently, 'a great selection of nearly-new furniture'. That was Eddie's kind of place. A store where you could see, and if you wanted to, buy, everything you needed at one go. One stop, no-nonsense shopping.

In a couple of hours in that saleroom on that one day, Eddie selected enough basic furniture for he and Nora to set up home with. There was a table and four chairs, a sideboard, two armchairs. And a bedroom suite with a double, solid wood, gentleman's wardrobe.

The whole lot cost him eighty pounds. Delivered.

The big test of the furniture, however, was, 'What will Nora think of it?' Eddie rang her to her work, and told her about his expedition, describing all the bits he had bought. Giving as much detail as he could remember. He was enthusiastic about it. Certainly, it would do him. But then he was a man, and easy to please in furniture. If he had a chair to sit on, a table to eat at, and a bed to sleep in, he would be happy.

But women were noted for being slightly more fussy. Caring about things like that.

Nora agreed to come up that evening and see it. What would her verdict be?

Eddie collected her, and brought her up to Quarry House, perched on the side of a gentle hill.

When he opened the door, his fiancee went ahead of him into the living room, in which Eddie had set out his purchases as tastefully as he possibly could.

There was silence for a few moments as Nora observed everything carefully. She sat in an armchair and surveyed the room. Then she rose, pulled out a chair and sat, elbows resting on the table. Slowly she allowed her fingertips to glide over its polished surface.

Eddie thought he saw the glint of a tear in her eye as she left the living room to go upstairs. To inspect the bedroom suite. Everything going well, so far, he thought.

Here again she looked carefully at every item. Opening the wardrobe door, she stuck her head into its cavernous depths. Then she bounced on the bed, to test the springs. Looked at herself, then over her shoulder at the waiting and wondering Eddie, in the mirror.

It was only when they were downstairs again, that Nora gave her considered opinion. Her summing up of the situation. Half-standing, half-sitting-on-her-hands on the edge of the sideboard, which was later to prove one of her favourite pieces in the whole house, she exclaimed, with genuine appreciation, "Oh Eddie, it's lovely. All lovely. I am so pleased with it!"

Eddie was so pleased too. And he also was appreciative.

To God. For His goodness. In bringing Nora and he together. And bringing things along, so well...

Getting married had been 'a good idea'.

The furniture was 'lovely'.

And now their wedding date had been arranged...

10

A PROMISE, A PREDICTION ...
AND A PROBLEM

❖

The little country Methodist Church on the outskirts of Caldbeck was full on Boxing Day, 26th December, 1951, for the wedding of Eddie and Nora. Family and friends had been invited as guests, and the people of both villages crowded in. It wasn't often that they were able to round off their Christmas festivities with the excitement of a wedding!

The marriage ceremony was conducted by Rev. Dennis Ferguson, and Richard and Betty, who had enjoyed so many happy times with Eddie and Nora, were their best man and bridesmaid on this happiest of happy times. It was a warm and touching occasion as the capacity congregation heard Eddie and Nora pledge to love and support each other. ''Til death do us part.'

Following the wedding service, all the guests moved across the village to Caldbeck Parish Hall for a reception. All kinds of home-made delights had been prepared, and there was much joy, and gladness. And a lot of sharing. Family and friends who only seemed to meet at weddings and funerals used this more pleasant of their two opportunities to catch up on all the latest news.

When everyone had eaten as much as they wanted, and chatted for as long as they were allowed, it was time for the speeches.

Time for the saying of all the polite, and wise, and wonderful things.

The thank-you-all-very-much things. And the wish-you-both-all-the-best things.

One of those who spoke was Mr. E.P. Brown, a friend of the Stobart family. And a Christian.

In the course of his speech, Mr. Brown had two significant points which he seemed anxious to get across to his by-now-relaxed and lazily listening audience.

The first was a promise which he claimed to have proved.

The second was an unusual prediction that he made.

The promise which he passed on to the young couple, setting out in life together, was a Scriptural one. It came from the Bible.

"I should just like to leave a promise with you, Eddie and Nora," he began. "It is taken from Proverbs chapter ten and verse twenty two. It says there, 'The blessing of the Lord it maketh rich, and he addeth no sorrow with it.' This is something which my wife and I have experienced in our own married life, and I would like to share it with the both of you.

Obviously you cannot experience the blessing of the Lord if you don't know Him. But you pair do. You have both come to trust Him, personally, for salvation. Now I would urge you to trust Him with your lives, unitedly. In everything you do, or even plan to do, put Him first. There is another verse in the Proverbs which tells us much the same thing. It says, 'In all thy ways acknowledge him, and he shall direct thy paths'. In other words, put Him first. In everything. And all the time. And if you do He will bless you, more than you could ever have imagined possible..."

Mr. Brown continued speaking for a few minutes, then concluded his remarks by making a peculiar prediction. What he really meant nobody knew, or understood, at the time. Perhaps he didn't even appreciate the full import of it himself.

Before the new husband, Eddie Stobart, had even bought a single lorry, E. P. Brown stood up at his wedding reception and stated, in all sincerity, "I am convinced that the Stobart name will go from the one end of this country to the other." Perhaps he recognised in the purposeful businessman Eddie, the entrepreneur that he was later to become.

After the reception was over, and Nora had changed out of her long wedding dress, the huggy-happy goodbyes were said and the newly-weds set off on their honeymoon. In Eddie's father's Morris 10, kindly lent and all shined up. Destination Capernwray Hall, in Lancashire. Sixty miles from Caldbeck.

It was in the deep mid-winter. And 'frosty winds made moan.'

During the day there had been a substantial fall of snow on the higher ground around the Lake District. And Eddie and Nora's route took them across some of that higher ground. Over Shap summit on the A6.

Having successfully negotiated the hills of Cumberland, the young married couple began the last leg of their journey to Capernwray Hall.

It was then that they were faced with their first major problem as husband and wife. They had a puncture!

Just as they went under a bridge on the outskirts of Carnforth, Eddie found steering very difficult. The left front wheel, he was soon to discover, was flat as a pancake!

Soon after his new wife had joined him at the front of the car and they had begun to discuss the problem, and contemplate their plight, shivering in their finery, a car drew up.

A middle-aged man got out of it and came back towards them.

"What's the problem?" he asked. "Can I help you?"

Eddie looked down at the pathetic-looking wheel and stated what must have been patently obvious. "We have a puncture," he replied.

The perceptive driver summed up the situation in a second. The good clothes. The confetti still sticking in Nora's hair. The facial expressions which were an intriguing blend of confusion, concern and contentment.

"You can't change a wheel tonight, sir!" he said to Eddie, with a twinkle in his eye. "I can see what you pair are up to! Where's your jack?"

While Eddie was rearranging his carefully packed boot in search of the jack, the complete stranger, who had by that time established his position beside the offending wheel, said to Nora, "Pass me the flashlight off the seat of my car, would you?"

When she had opened the door of the car, Nora noticed that there was a book lying on the passenger seat. Beside the 'flashlight'. A second glance confirmed that the book was indeed a well-worn Bible.

In less than half-an-hour the kind motorist had the relieved couple safely on their way again.

As they both climbed into the car to complete their journey Eddie and Nora were so grateful to God, and to this man who was probably a fellow-Christian, for their help.

The man's final words as he waved to them as the car drove off were a wish and a prayer all in one.

"May God bless you both!" he called.

Much later that evening Mr. and Mrs. Eddie Stobart arrived, very tired, but very content at Capernwray Hall. To begin their honeymoon.

It was to be the first night of a fruitful life. Together.

11

ONLY THE BEST WILL DO

❖

When the new husband and wife partnership returned from the relaxation and spiritual battery-recharge of their honeymoon in Capernwray Hall they moved straight into their first home at Quarry House, Brocklebank, Wigton.

Eddie went straight back to work in his farm contracting business. And Nora found plenty to do in the house. Eddie had done the furnishing. Now it was left to her to do the finishing.

When their first child, little daughter Anne, was born, late in 1952, the pair became even happier. And busier! Daddy worked harder to support his wife and their first baby, and Nora had the pleasure, and responsibility of caring for her.

It was great.

About a year later, when Nora was expecting their second child, the young couple decided that they would like to raise their increasing family in a home with more 'facilities'. And if possible, somewhere that was their own. Although the rent of Quarry House was a mere 12/6 (62p) per week the amenities in the draughty farmhouse could only be described as 'basic'.

So they looked around for somewhere to buy. The only property on the market at that time, that suited their requirements, they discovered, was a bungalow at Newlands Hill. After a few preliminary inspections, and some discussion as to how they were going to raise the purchase price, Eddie and Nora decided to buy that bungalow.

It would give them more room. And it would be a reasonably safe place in which to raise a family.

The purchase price was agreed at four hundred and fifty pounds. Eddie was able to raise the first fifty pounds of this amount by way of a deposit, and he arranged a loan with a Building Society for the remainder. This loan was granted on the condition that Eddie undertook to install a hot water supply, and build on a bathroom. Both within one year.

When the Stobart family moved into Newlands Hill in November, 1953, there were four of them. Little Anne had by then acquired a baby brother, John, who was only six weeks old.

During the following winter months it was marvellous to enjoy the relative comfort of a bungalow, with all its rooms on the one floor. Toddler Anne had terrific fun, stomping from one room into another, down the long side corridor to the bedrooms. The layout of the bungalow reminded Nora, when she first saw it, of the railway carriages she used to travel in, to and from Lockerbie at the weekends!

The bungalow was good. But it could be better.

Terms had been agreed. Improvements had to be made.

Eddie knew that he would have to employ the services of a building contractor to do the necessary work. He was handy enough with motors and machines himself, but he had no experience whatsoever of things like plumbing and plastering.

On making a few enquiries, Eddie was given the name of a local contractor who was reputed to be 'both honest and reliable'. The kind of man he liked.

He approached this builder, told him what he wanted, satisfied himself that he could do the job. Then employed him.

When the renovation work began it proved to be a much bigger job than had been at first anticipated. For in addition to building on a bathroom, and plumbing the whole bungalow, the conscientious workman saw other improvements which could, and he reckoned should, be made.

The living room fireplace needed replaced. And so too did a substantial section of the roof.

When he told the young first-time-buyers with the growing family of his recommendations they could see his point. The repairs which he had outlined were sensible. Essential, probably. But although they could see his point they could also see their own problem.

How were they ever going to be able to pay for what amounted to a major reconstruction project on their bungalow?

"Never worry," the builder replied when Eddie voiced their concerns to him one day. "Never worry. I will do the work that needs to be done, then we can talk again about payment when it is finished. In the meantime, though, if it makes it easier for you, just give me what you can, when you can."

The truth was that this particular man liked working at Newlands Hill. He knew Eddie to be an honest and hardworking contractor. Like himself, but in a different line of work. And he liked the friendly family atmosphere about the place, too.

He took great delight in poking gentle fun at the rapidly maturing Anne, whose self-appointed task seemed to be to tell him when the next cup of tea was ready.

"Here comes Anne, my old tea-pot, again!" he would joke.

Eddie tried to help this very reliable and generous workman as often, and as best as he could. To help minimise expenses. And it was in that man that Eddie saw practised, and from him that he heard reiterated, the principles in which John Millican had instructed him that summer night seven or eight years earlier. In a solar-heated greenhouse.

There were times, though, when Eddie reckoned that he went 'over the top' a bit. He was just far too fussy. Take the fitting of the new grate, for instance. Before the new fireplace was even brought near the yawning hole in the living-room wall all the preparations for it had to be thoroughly carried out. To Eddie, who was eventually going to have to pay for all this fussing about, it all seemed rather unnecessary. The man was doing exactly what John Millican had advised the disappointed and disgruntled young thresher-operator to do. The best job possible.

When Eddie began helping his friend on the roof, he was somewhat slow at first. He crawled up the roof on all fours. And he just carried the replacement slates up to the versatile workman as they turned up in the pile.

So the experienced contractor gave his assistant some encouragement. And some words of wisdom, as well.

The encouragement came when he told Eddie, "Get up on your feet man, and **walk** up the roof! You won't fall. You will find it a lot easier." Gingerly, Eddie tried it. And found he could do it. And the builder was right, too. It did make the carrying of slates a lot easier!

After he had carried up a number of only-slightly-defective slates, Eddie had them handed back to him with the comment, "Don't bring me any damaged or chipped or badly-shaped slates, son. I won't be putting them on your roof."

Then, as the work progressed, Eddie carried up a slate that seemed O.K. to him. The roofer looked at it, carefully. After turning it over in his hand, disapprovingly, two or three times, he looked his helper straight in the eye. "If you bring me up any more bad slates, Eddie, I will start throwing them back at you," he said. "Only the best will do."

For a while Eddie checked all the slates he was carrying up to the perfectionist on the roof of his bungalow. And the work progressed apace. Then, all of a sudden, when half-way up with another load, Eddie saw the builder take a long hard look down at the ground. He was, as Eddie was soon to discover, merely checking that there was nothing, or more importantly, nobody, in his line of fire.

With a deft flick of his wrist, he launched the heavy slate, which flew down past the baffled Eddie and smashed into smithereens in the yard.

When he looked up from the remains of a slate to the man who had thrown it, Eddie noticed that there was a wry smile playing around the corners of his mouth. Shaking his head in a how-many-times-am-I-going-to-have-tell-you? manner he remarked, calmly, "It doesn't seem to have got through to you yet, Eddie. Only the best will do!"

For four months that man worked around Newlands Hill, completely refurbishing the bungalow, both inside and out. He witnessed some changes in the family in that time, too. Anne, his 'old teapot', and John were becoming more interesting by the day.

After the first month everyone had begun to regard the man whose sole mision in life appeared to be the pulling-out and putting-back, the knocking down and building-up of great chunks of their home, as an old friend. Part of the furniture. One of the family. It seemed as though he belonged, somehow. Had always been around.

So it was strange when the afternoon came when he reckoned that he was finished. Everything that needed to be done, had been done. And well.

On that afternoon, Eddie and he discussed the matter of payment, once more.

The contractor's response was much the same as it had been before.

"I have done a good job for you, Eddie. Indeed, an excellent job," he declared. "I realised, when I saw the amount of work that needed to be done to this place, that you would never be able to pay me for it, all at once. But I know you. And I trust you. You pay me what you can. When you can. I don't care if it takes you two, or three, or even four years..."

He then took off his cap and gave his forehead a wipe with the sleeve of his overall before delivering his final piece of advice. "But I want you always to remember this, Eddie," he went on. "You will get over paying for a good job, but a bad one you will never get over. Ever."

Something more for Eddie to remember. The words of wisdom for the days ahead were mounting up.

"You will get over paying for a good job..."

"Be sure to put your trust in God..."

"Always leave the stackyard tidy..."

And of course, the practical lesson of the shattered slate, "Only the best will do!"

12

THE GUY AT THE GARAGE

❖

As Eddie Stobart, with his father and brother, had continued to work away in their farm contracting business, so it had continued to grow.

Eddie's father, when threshing for farmers, saw an opportunity for expansion. As he moved around the countryside, from one farmyard to another, he discovered that there were farmers who had harvested more hay, straw or grain than they would ever need. And there were others who told him with some concern, "You know, John, I don't think I'm going to have enough feeding and bedding to see me through the winter."

John had a very simple idea. Obvious, it seemed to him. He had contact with a great number of farmers, and they shared with him the state of their stocks. He would buy from those who had a surplus. And sell to those with a shortage. Easy. And it worked!

In order to advance this business venture it became obvious that a lorry would be an essential item of equipment. So one was purchased. Then, with Ronnie doing most of the driving, and Eddie helping when he was available, John Stobart started to trade in hay, straw and grain, all over Cumberland. Then, as farmers heard of his buy-from-you-and-sell-to-him service, they asked him to buy in stocks for them. So he was compelled to extend his borders, and purchase from farmers farther afield. All over the north of England.

It was at this time that Eddie Stobart realized that the farm contracting business, with all three of them in it, father, brother and himself was becoming too big. And unmanageable. It was a family affair, with three men working as hard as they could. Doing what needed to be done, wherever it needed to be done.

With his neat and tidy mind and nature, Eddie began to want to see things more clearly defined. So he talked to Ronnie about it, and he agreed. Yes. It would be better if everyone knew who was doing what. When. And for whom. Then everybody could see what was happening. But there was an even more pressing reason that was constraining Eddie to urge for a complete clarification of the whole situation.

It was late in 1957. Eddie was now twenty-eight years of age and had a wife and three children to support. Little Edward had been born three years before and with sister Anne and brother John made Eddie and Nora's family complete. Or so they thought!

Back at the home farm, Bankdale Head, too, there were now six young children to be cared for. Dorothy and Isobel had joined their two older brothers, and two older sisters, to complete John and Ruth's family.

If Ronnie and his father operated out of Bankdale Head, carrying on trading in hay, straw and grain, Eddie had seen an opening for him to branch out into something new. Something completely different. Yet again.

In the late 1950's the arrival and increased use of that rumbling giant of field and farm, the combine harvester, had led to the gradual demise of the threshing machine. However, as one thing was declining, so another was increasing. This was the use of machinery to spread basic slag on the fields as fertiliser.

With an eye that was able to spot, and an uncanny knack for grasping, a worthwhile opportunity as soon as it popped up, Eddie recognised that this was the way things were going. And if things were going that way, he was going that way, too!

John Stobart and his two oldest sons met one day so that they could divide out the business interests. 'Give unto' Eddie 'the portion of goods that falleth unto him', as the Bible puts it.

After some discussion and examination of who had, and did what, it was decided that Eddie's share of the family 'estate' should be as follows :-

1	Thresher	£150 - 00
1	Fordson tractor	£250 - 00
1	Nuffield tractor	£150 - 00
	Fuel tanks	£ 50 - 00
	Cash in hand	£100 - 00
	Total assets	£700 -00

Father John and brother Ronnie expressed themselves happy with that agreement. And Eddie was happy with it, too.

He was ready to establish a business, on his own, now, with machinery in the yard. Some money in the bank. His faith in God. Experience in his hands. And his head crammed full of sound and practical advice!

When he first started out in the spreading-basic-slag-for-fertiliser business, Eddie worked for the local agricultural merchants. They took the orders from the farmers, and supplied the raw materials. Then Eddie undertook to spread it on the fields. All around the countryside.

Initially he had worked for a number of merchants, but then discovered that he had more work than he could possibly do. After a number of months he found that the well-known firm of Harrison Ivinson of Caldbeck could supply him with sufficient orders to keep him busy. So he began to work solely for them.

As with every business one needs the proper equipment. The right tools to do the job. A threshing machine wasn't much use to a man spreading slag!

It would be necessary to make some changes. Thus, in 1960, Eddie sold the thresher and bought a brand new fertiliser spreader which cost £475. This seemed a lot of money to him at the time, but then what was it that they had all been saying? Things like, Do the best job you can. Or, only the best will do. And that meant using the proper machinery. All the time. And every time.

Now that the family were beginning to grow up, Eddie and Nora needed some way of getting them all about. To church. To school. To shop. So Eddie looked around. Asked around. And dealt around.

Then he bought their first family car. It was an Austin Seven. For £35. How everybody loved to pack into that little car and travel around the Cumbrian countryside! That was when Daddy wasn't working, of course!

For Daddy Eddie was becoming busier and busier. As with the threshing, so with the spreading. When the word got around that Eddie Stobart was 'spreading for Harrison Ivinson now', and that he did 'a good job', an increasing number of farmers arranged for him to fertilise their fields.

He wasn't long in the business, either, until Eddie found that he was lacking one basic item of equipment. He required something in which to transport the fertiliser from source to site. From storage yard to farmyard.

In short, he needed a lorry.

At different times, early or late in the day, or between spreading jobs, Eddie began making a few enquiries. Around garages and depots. Finding out what was on the market. And at what price.

Trouble was though, he didn't tell Nora where he had been. Or what he had seen. She knew that he 'was looking for a lorry'. From somewhere. But she didn't know just where.

One day the phone rang at Newlands Hill.

The busy wife and mother answered it.

"Is Eddie there?" enquired a man's voice at the other end of the line.

"No, I'm afraid he's not here at the minute," Nora replied. "Can I take a message?"

"I was wondering if he is still interested in this Guy down at the garage?" came the caller's next question.

Nora was stumped. Completely.

Being generally, though not totally, ignorant of lorry makes and matters at that time, and thinking that perhaps her husband had been considering employing more staff, another 'guy', she thought for a moment. Then she continued hesitantly, sounding rather mystified, "Who? What guy? What's his name?"

There was a sudden silence on the line.

Then a loud laugh.

"This Guy isn't a man, Missus!" the garage-owner made no attempt to conceal his amusement. "It's a LORRY!"

Nora was embarrassed, but she saw the joke. After apologising for her ignorance she agreed to pass on the message. About the right Guy.

When Eddie came home she told him the story. He, too, had a laugh at her expense, then off he went. To see the Guy at the garage.

As what he saw pleased him, Eddie bought that Guy Invincible four-wheeler truck. It would be ideal for transporting basic slag.

In a few week's time the whole truck had been carefully repainted in Eddie's choice of colours. Post-office red and Brunswick green. And the lettering on both doors of the cab said simply :-

E. P. STOBART
Caldbeck 206
Cumberland.

The first Eddie Stobart lorry was on the road!

13

A DIFFICULT DECISION

❖

Everything seemed to be going well. The business was sailing along just fine. A new fertiliser spreader. A new car. A new lorry. And plenty of work. Eddie was kept busy, and when he was busy he was happy, from morning to night, every single working day...

Then suddenly, totally unexpectedly, trouble loomed on the horizon. A sudden squall blew up. To almost sink the boat.

Out of the blue, and without anyone having the slightest inkling of what was going to happen, Harrison Ivinson went out of business. Stopped trading. Overnight. Just like that!

This created massive problems for Eddie and his basic slag spreaders, and spreading. He had men to pay, machinery to maintain, and worse than either of those, hefty hire purchase payments to honour. And no work.

Suddenly, all at one fell swoop, all the orders which he had would become impossible to fulfil.

Harrison Ivinson had ceased to be. And so had all his pending jobs. He was unable to just take over the business himself because one required a licence to become an agricultural merchant. A licence which Eddie didn't have. And would find it difficult to obtain. Or so he was told, when he enquired into it, in mild but mounting desperation.

To make matters worse, the whole family, all five of them, were living in a caravan in the yard at Newlands Hill at the time. Nora was expecting their fourth child, and they had decided to build an extension to their bungalow and make some other alterations as well.

As though the inconvenience of five people in a cramped caravan on a wet day with the rain running down the outsides of the windows and the condensation running down the insides of the windows wasn't enough to cope with. Now they had this. And the worry of it all.

The alterations and extension to their home had been undertaken on the strength of a flourishing business. A full order book. And lots to to. Now he still had a full order book. But he had nothing to do. For his sole source of supply for basic slag had dried up. How could Eddie ever satisfy his farmer-customers? And how were they ever going to be able to pay the ever-growing pile of bills?

Eddie and Nora talked about the situation, often. It was a difficult dilemma for a young couple with a young family. What could they do?

After some anxious thought and a lot of discussion and consultation with others, Eddie decided that the only way out for him was to form a company, apply for a licence and take over the Harrison Ivinson franchise.

With this aim in view he approached three prominent businessmen who agreed to join him as directors of such a company. They liked the idea, regarding it as an extremely viable proposition. And preparations went ahead, apace.

The necessary capital to establish a new company had been found, a name for the new enterprise had been chosen, the statutory legal documents were in the process of being finalised, when something else happened.

God intervened in the life of Eddie Stobart.

From his early back-of-the-B.S.A.-with-daddy days, Eddie had been a regular attender at the annual Keswick Convention in July. In those boyhood days he had gone for the motor-bike ride and the multi-cultural experience. Latterly, however, as a Christian married man, he always went a number of times. To hear the Word of God and meet other Christians. It was, for him, a time of spiritual challenge and refreshment.

So when the Convention came around in 1961, and Eddie was not as busy at his work as he would dearly like to have been, he and Nora went along to the massive tent in Keswick on a Thursday afternoon.

Going into the tent, it was just like any other year. The music playing, the people from all parts of the world coming and going, smiling, talking, greeting one another. Praising God. Sharing their experiences. And their faith...

No matter how often he had been, and he had been many times, Eddie always loved to soak up the amiable atmosphere of the Convention.

The speaker that afternoon, Rev. Herbert Cragg, took as his text 2 Corinthians 6 v.14, 'Be ye not unequally yoked with unbelievers: for what fellowship hath righteousness with unrighteousness? and what communion hath light with darkness?'

When he heard the text announced and read, Eddie felt slightly uncomfortable. But only slightly. Perhaps the speaker would have an interesting interpretation of the verse. A novel slant on it.

However, that didn't happen. On the contrary, when Herbert Cragg began to speak, Eddie was convinced that he was speaking directly to, and at, him.

"I am not going to be talking about the unequal yoke in the marriage bond, today, though that is often done from this particular passage of Scripture," he began by proclaiming. "I feel God would have me speak to you this afternoon about unequal partnerships in business."

And he did just that. Powerfully.

When he announced his particular choice of emphasis for that meeting, and as he proceeded to develop the subject throughout his sermon, Eddie was sure that the preacher was looking down at him. With every word. He felt that he was the reason for the message. It was as though an arrow had gone clean through him and embedded itself in the back of his seat. Pinning him there.

He was captured. Captivated. Awestruck.

Had this man heard of his business dealings? His soon-to-be-partnership in a soon-to-be company?

No. He couldn't have. Nohow.

If the speaker hadn't known of his latest proposed enterprise, then there was only one answer to his choice of topic, Eddie reckoned.

It could be none other than the voice of God. To him.

As he sat in that meeting, spellbound, in a state of spiritual shock, Eddie considered his options.

There could be no doubt whatsoever that God had been speaking to him. But did that mean he couldn't or shouldn't enter into a partnership with these other men? He knew of others, believers, whose life and testimony he greatly respected, who were linked in various ways with non-Christians. If it was all right for them, why shouldn't it be all right for him?

He struggled with that one for a while, then came to the conclusion that every Christian was responsible to God for his or her own actions. Each individual believer acted as he felt that God was leading him at the time. And would be judged by God, accordingly. So he shouldn't be measuring himself against others. Making them an excuse for himself. That was just an easy way out. An emergency exit.

This matter was between himself and God. And nobody else.

And he couldn't escape it. Those words kept echoing in his ears, haunting him, 'Be ye not unequally yoked with unbelievers.'

On the way home in the car Eddie shared his thoughts and concerns with his wife. Nora, too, had been moved by the message that afternoon.

She had heard it through her husband's ears.

Had felt it stinging her husband's heart.

Had applied it in her husband's situation.

They agreed to pray about the matter, asking God for guidance as to Eddie's next move.

That was a no-sleep night for him. He tumbled and tossed, and planned and prayed.Then made a courageous choice...

Next morning Eddie rang his other would-be partners and told them that it was all off. When they asked for, and were given, the reason for this sudden-about-turn decision, they were completely baffled. What had religion got to do with business, anyway? they wondered, then asked, rather pointedly.

Despite their annoyance, Eddie had made up his mind. He wasn't prepared to enter into that particular partnership. He believed that God had warned him against it. In a very direct way.

He would go it alone, with his faith in Him. Whatever the cost.

It was a brave and bold conclusion to come to.

For now he had all his commitments. All his repayments.

With no work.

And no prospect of any.

His chances of ever fulfilling his orders to his Harrison Ivinson clients had gone for good.

He thought...

14

"THOSE WHO HONOUR ME ..."

❖

After the dramatic make-your-mind-up events of the Thursday at the Convention, and the Friday on the telephone, Eddie went into Carlisle, on the next day, the Saturday. In fact he had been going into Carlisle every Saturday for many years. For a particular reason. And he saw no need to stop now. Even though he was in a bit of a fix.

Saturday was farm auction day in the city. Since farmers from all over north Cumberland and the borders gravitated towards that event, it became a regular place for Eddie to rendezvous with them. It was an excellent location in which to obtain orders for farm work. Like threshing. Or spreading fertiliser.

While walking around the auction mart that day, chatting to the farming fraternity, Eddie was beset by a strange cocoction of concerns. He had a clear conscience, sure enough, for he never had any doubt but that he had made the right decision. But he also had a mixed-up mind and a heavy heart.

As the morning progressed, however, Eddie was astonished to discover that nearly every farmer he spoke to gave him an order. For basic slag to be spread on their fields. By him. Eddie. And nobody else. By early afternoon he had more orders than he had ever received in one day in his life. And the day was by no means over yet!

To each of the farmers, many of whom were long-established customers, Eddie patiently explained his dilemma. "I will take your order," he told them, "But you see I have a problem with it. Since Harrison Ivinson's have closed down, I have no way of obtaining basic slag, in bulk. You need a licence to do that, apparently. And I haven't got one. So I don't know how I am going to get the slag to meet all these demands."

Then he would conclude by flicking through , for the benefit of his would-be customer, or small group of would-be customers, the steadily increasing collection of orders in his hand.

No matter to whom, or to how many, Eddie made his I'm-not-a-merchant-for-I-don't-have-a-licence apologetic explanation, the response was always the same. It was so invariable that it became pleasingly predictable. "Do what you want, Eddie," came the reply, again and again. "Do what you must. But just don't forget, it is **you** that we want to do our work!"

There were two auction marts in Carlisle and Eddie kept crossing from one to the other in the course of any one Saturday. Experience had taught him who would be where, and when, so he always made sure that he was in the best possible position to pick up the best posible selection of orders.

To make this one-mart-to-the-other short trip Eddie usually passed the door of a firm called Oliver and Snowden, whose main business interest was the sale of agricultural machinery. This company had been selling some bagged fertiliser, but they had never dealt in bulk supply. That had been the exclusive domain of Harrison Ivenson. Who were by now no more.

Whilst making one of his mart-to-mart-excursions, in mid-afternoon, Eddie decided, on an impulse, as he thought, but guided by God, as it was to turn out, to call in and have a word with the manager, whom he knew to be a Mr. Colson. The farm contractor had seen this Mr. Colson about the firm when he had been in dealing for machinery. He didn't expect the busy manager to know who he was though.

It came as somewhat of a surprise then to Eddie when Mr. Colson ushered him into his office, offered him a chair, and then addressed him by name!

Seating himself comfortably in his own armchair behind a well-worn wooden desk, he looked Eddie straight in the eye and said, with a quaint smile, "Aye, young Stobart. I know what you've come for!"

Eddie was puzzled. Here was somebody else who seemed to know as much about him as he knew himself!

"What have I come for then?" Eddie asked, testing him.

"You have come in here to see if we are interested in taking over your involvment in Harrison Ivinson's business, I'm quite sure," he replied with a sickeningly smug, correct-me-if-I'm-wrong expression.

"I have to admit that you are dead right", Eddie had no choice but to concede. "I have come in to see if there is any way in which you could help me out with my customers."

There was a silence. Mr. Colson was still regarding the ambitious young businessman across his office. He broke the stillness every now and again by tapping out short bursts of rhythm with his left hand on the desk. From little finger to thumb in quick succession. The fingers made a sharp click. The thumb a dull thud.

Since he was obviously not going to make any comment, much more commit himself to anything, yet, Eddie went on, "Well, now that you know what I'm in here for, what will your answer be? What do you think?" he enquired.

Mr. Colson appeared interested. At least he hadn't said 'No' immediately. And that was always something.

His considered answer, to Eddie's eager questioning, when it came, was cautious. "I couldn't tell you what my answer will be. I would need to know more about what it is that you are proposing, before I give you any answer," he replied.

That was understandable, Eddie reckoned.

So he then went on to tell the manager about his dilemma upon the collapse of Harrison and Ivinson. His full order book. And his inability to procure the slag to honour those orders. Then, to press home his point, he spread out before him the sheaf of orders which he had taken that very day.

The man at the desk thumbed through them, idly. There were farmers amongst them who were well known to him. He mentioned a few of the names, audibly, saying things like,"Oh, so you know Colin Cornstack," or,

"And you work for Tommy Thingamee, as well"...

Eddie sat quietly, considering it unwise to interrupt such meaningful meditation.

It so happened that a fair number of the farmers from whom Eddie had taken orders were also amongst Oliver and Snowden's most reliable customers.

Mr. Colson appeared impressed, now.

After they had chatted the situation through, generally, for ten or fifteen minutes, Eddie rose and made for the door. He had made it clear to the man what he had come in for. And he didn't want to take up any more of his time. Especially on a busy Saturday afternoon.

It was then that Mr. Colson gave his response. The best he possibly could in the circumstances.

"I will let you know what decision we come to, Eddie," he promised. "But mind you it might be some time before I am able to get back to you. The other directors are all busy men, and they live a good distance away, so it will take me a while to get in touch with them".

That was encouraging, at least.

Eddie would know something. Sometime.

He had an easier mind, and a lighter heart when he came out of that shop. So much so, indeed, that he continued along to the mart which had been his intended destination, and collected another handful of orders!

Then, to crown the day, just as he arrived back home at Newlands Hill, shortly after five o'clock, the phone was ringing in his office. He had barely time to speak to Nora or the children before going in to answer it.

It came as quite a surprise to him to find Mr. Colson at the other end of the line. Eddie had thought that his 'some time to get back to you' had meant days. Or even weeks. Certainly not hours.

"I have phoned all the other directors about your proposition, Eddie, and they are all in full agreement," was the message which he had obviously been instructed to convey. "If you could be back at my office here at nine o'clock on Monday morning we will go along to the solicitors and have some papers drawn up. Then you can carry on with your work".

Eddie was thrilled.

The God who had spoken to him on Thursday, had honoured his difficult decision of Friday by turning his life around in a totally different direction on Saturday.

And a whole new phase in the life of Eddie Stobart was set to begin.

On Monday.

15

UP, OUT AND AT IT
ALL OF YOU!

❖

In response to Mr. Colson's invitation, Eddie turned up, all shined up, in the premises of Oliver and Snowden, Carlisle, early on the Monday morning. He had spent Sunday praising God for His goodness and obvious guidance. Now he was all set to spend Monday preparing himself for busy days ahead.

There was much work to be done. Many orders to be met. Men to be kept employed.

Eddie wanted to be up, and out, and at it. As soon as possible.

Mr. Colson greeted him in a friendly but businesslike fashion. He didn't have a lot of time to waste lounging around talking about the weather, either.

"If you are ready, Eddie, I think we should go along to Burnetts, the solicitors, and draw up a contract," he proposed.

Eddie was ready for that. Was that not why he had come?

After some discussion of various points of practice, a contract was drawn up between Oliver and Snowden, agricultural merchants, and Eddie Stobart, contractor.

Since they had a licence to handle such work, Oliver and Snowden were to be responsible for the taking of all the orders from the farmers, for fertiliser. Eddie, in turn, was to take responsibility for the collection of the basic slag from the steelworks, where it was in fact a residue, a waste product of the smelting process, and tranport it to Cumberland. Then, using his men and machines, he was to spread it on the farmers' fields.

Eddie was pleased with this contract. It gave him tremendous freedom to develop and expand his part of the operation. Yet, wise after the event, he was scared of a second collapse. More sleepless nights and unemployed men. So he was careful to ensure that there were safeguards written into this new contract to cover such unlikely but always remotely possible eventualities.

From he left the solicitor's office that morning, Eddie began to work harder than ever. There were so many farmers just waiting for him to fertilise their fields...

By this time the 'Guy from the garage' had been traded in against two Ford Thames Trader trucks, which were again painted in Eddie's favourite red and green. And they carried his logo on the cab doors, as the original Guy had done. Eddie also had six men employed, operating three spreaders.

The essential element in the whole set-up, the raw material, the basic slag, had to be collected by the two E.P. Stobart lorries from the steelworks in any one of three different locations. Middlesbrough in North Yorkshire, Scunthorpe in Lincolnshire, or Corby, Northants.

Scunthorpe and Corby were each a day's run for a driver, but since the steelworks in Middlesbrough was a mere one hundred miles from the Stobart yard, Eddie did that run himself, often, early in the morning.

Many, many times he rose at four a.m. and sat quietly on the edge of the bed. He wanted to slip out and away without awakening his wife. Nora had plenty to think about during the day, so she would be better asleep when he was out, rumbling round the roads in the early hours, he reckoned.

When her rhythmic and regular respiration reassured him that she was still far off in the land of dreams, he crept furtively along the hallway, and snatched something to eat in the kitchen. Then he stole silently out to a waiting lorry, closing the cab door with a careful clunk rather than a boisterous bang.

His only fear was that the noise of the engine, as it roared into life, would awaken Nora or some of the children. But even if it did, they were warm and comfortable in bed. All they had to do was go back to sleep again.

And he was away! Out on the silent traffic-free road to Middlesbrough. He would be there, have his load collected and be back to Cumberland in time to have it spread on the fields that day. And in time, too, for another driver to take the lorry on to Scunthorpe or Corby!

On his way home Eddie invariably stopped in a telephone kiosk on the A66, just outside Penrith, and told Nora that he was nearly home. Again.

She knew that it would take him half-an-hour to make it home from there. And she would have something prepared for him to eat. He was usually ravenous!

It seemed to Eddie that he had been awake for a long time by then. Yet he hadn't even started the real day's work!

As the flow of orders coming through from Oliver and Snowden, agricultural merchants, steadily increased, Eddie was compelled to employ more men. And with an increased number of drivers and helpers came the problem of moving those workmen from place to place. Site to site. Farm to farm. Field to field. And they had to be left out to the farm where the spreaders were working on any particular day. Then collected from there, or perhaps somewhere else, in the evening.

To overcome this problem, Eddie bought a Ford Transit van, and since he and his other employees were often busily engaged on some other job, Nora doubled up as the unofficial 'driver'.

This extra 'job' for her was not made any easier when a fourth Stobart child, William, was born in November, 1961. Eddie and she had, for years, believed their family to be complete, for Edward was, by then, a boy of seven, running around.

But obviously it wasn't!

Not that he knew very much about it at the time, but little William, who did prove to be the youngest of the family, had an early introduction to the workings of the Eddie Stobart business enterprise. (E.P. had by then become Eddie on all of the lorries.)

When his mother had to deliver men to a work location in the morning, or move them from farm to farm during the day, and her older children, Anne, John and Edward were at school, she tucked number four up in his carry-cot, and laid him across the long front seat in the van beside her. And off they went! Round the lattice work of roads and lanes in rural Cumberland. From one farmer's field to another farmer's field.

To do their bit!

And keep the work progressing!

16

JUST BOIL THEM SOME 'TATTIES'

❖

It was in the spring of 1963 when, one typically busy morning, a Triumph Herald arrived in the yard at Newlands Hill. The driver, a well-dressed middle-aged gentleman, had the air of somebody searching for somebody, or something, but not quite sure whether he had found him, or her, or it, yet. As he stepped out of the car one would have assumed by his dapper appearance that he was the kind of a gent who would be more familiar with finance than fertiliser. With stocks and shares rather than basic slag.

Eddie approached the man who by that time was looking all around him with more than merely a mild curiosity. He was wondering, probably, if he had found who or what it was that he was looking for, at last.

"Would you, by any chance be Mr. Eddie Stobart?" he enquired immediately, anxious to end his quest.

"I am indeed," Eddie replied, wiping his hands on a duster. "What can I do for you?"

Glancing into the stranger's car as he spoke, Eddie noticed that there was an Ordinance survey map of north Cumberland lying in a half-open-half-folded heap on the passenger seat.

Strange, he thought. Not a lot of people go to that kind of lengths to find us!

As he was soon to discover, however, the map the man had been carrying, and had obviously consulted, had been used for a far more specific reason than simply to find his way. But he had used it for that secondary purpose, too, no doubt.

The man-in-the-suit was aware that Eddie was puzzled as to why he was there, so he lost no more time before explaining his presence in the yard at Newlands Hill.

He introduced himself first.

"My name is Buchanan," he began, "and I am a representative for the agricultural division of the chemical manufacturers, I.C.I."

That was the man. Now for his mission.

"I have come, on behalf of the company, to locate exactly where you live, and what facilities you have here. You see, Mr. Stobart, you are living right in the centre of an agricultural area where we want to set up a basic slag store," he said.

"We would pay you to bring in the slag," he went on. "And if you agree to help us we will pay you for handling it. And for storing it, as well."

It was a pleasant morning, and Eddie leaned against the side of the Triumph Herald, considering this all-of-a-sudden and out-of-the-blue proposition.

He was just that little bit cautious. It all sounded a bit too good to be true to him. Here was as man, standing in his yard, telling him that they were going to pay him for doing what he had been doing for the previous two years, at his own expense!

There must be a snag in it somewhere, he concluded.

"What would be required of me, then, in return for all of this?" he asked, knowing that he would be expected to do something, or provide something. Sometime or somehow. As far as he could remember, I.C.I. were not a registered charity.

"We would want you to provide us with a building that would hold 6,000 tons of basic slag. You would be required to supply the site, somewhere around here, obtain planning permission for a store, erect the building, and set up a weighbridge," Eddie's visitor told him.

Not a lot when you said it quickly. All in the one breath, as he had done. Just like that!

Despite the niggling realization at the back of his mind, that somewhere along the line this whole enterprise was going to cost money before it made money, Eddie recognised in it yet another wonderful opportunity for expansion. And he liked opportunities for expansion.

"It all sounds good to me," he replied, after a few minutes as-careful-as-he-could-carry-out-in-the-circumstances consideration. "If I agree to put up a slag store around here, what is the next step?"

Mr. Buchanan knew what the next step was. He didn't need to puzzle long over that one. He had worked it all out, weeks before. Every possible reaction to every possible response. Each stage as it came.

"The next step," he continued, "is for me to bring two of my superiors from the company down here to Newlands Hill, from Edinburgh, to have a look around. They would have to inspect the site, meet you, and satisfy themselves that everything was in order before a deal could be finalised."

That was fair enough to Eddie. Acceptable, reasonable, business procedure.

"Could we meet in a hotel round here, soon, and have lunch together? Then we could spend the afternoon surveying the site, discussing terms and conditions and so on," the rep. from I.C.I. suggested.

"That's O.K. by me," Eddie replied. "We can meet anytime you like, but not at a hotel. We will meet here, in our house, and my wife will make the dinner. Then we can spend as long as it takes to discuss everything. Here on site."

A date and time for their next meeting was thus agreed upon, and Mr. Buchanan, representative from I.C.I., drove off. Well-satisfied. It had been a successful morning's work, he reckoned.

When Eddie went into the house, Nora was naturally curious to discover what the 'long conversation with the man in the yard' had all been about.

Her husband recounted to her all that Mr. Buchanan had told him. About I.C.I. and their need for a slag store. About how they just happened to be living bang in the centre of the company's proposed development area. Not forgetting the point of the whole exercise. How that he had been asked about his willingness to undertake the erection of a slag store, and the drawing in of the basic slag.

All very interesting.

Then he told her about the dinner which he had suggested that she could make for Mr. Buchanan and his bosses.

Nora was pleased for her husband and his plans for development. But she was not just so pleased with him and his plans for dinner.

"What on earth will I make them for dinner, Eddie?" she asked him, apprehensively. Half-angry, half-anxious. "These will be top men. Big bosses. Used to dining high. Why did you not agree to go with them to a hotel when the man suggested it? What could I give them that they would be used to eating?"

Eddie knew his wife. And her dinners. She could cook and present a lovely meal. But she underestimated herself. Was always worried in case the meal wasn't big enough, or warm enough, or fancy enough...

"Give them your usual, Nora," he replied calmly, in an effort to keep his wife calm, too. "Just boil them some 'tatties'. With roast beef and Yorkshire pudding. What could be any better than that?"

When the big day came, the day that Eddie and Nora had both planned carefully for, in totally different ways, and for totally different reasons, three men from I.C.I. arrived in time for a midday meal. As arranged.

There was Mr. Thornleigh, a senior executive with the company's agricultural division, from Edinburgh, Mr. Goldie, one of his assistant managers, and Mr. Buchanan. The man with the Triumph Herald. The person who had done the groundwork, and set up the meeting.

When Nora had served the meal, all five of them sat down around the dining-room table. Before they began to eat, however, Eddie, whose practice had always been to thank God for all His provision for both his spiritual and physical needs, said softly, "We will just say grace and ask God's blessing on what we are doing here today."

The three visitors, who may not have been used to such customs, sat quietly, with heads bowed, as their host thanked God for the food. And asked His guidance in their deliberations of later in the afternoon.

Nora needn't have worried about the meal. At all. Everyone enjoyed it. And said so.

Then, although the meal had been spent in an atmosphere of amicable conversation the afternoon was spent in serious discussion. The men from I.C.I examined every avenue of the proposed basic slag store with the man who had some years of experince in the handling of that very material, Eddie Stobart.

Although they didn't tell Eddie of their decision, there and then, promising that he would hear from them, 'soon, by post', that senior management team were ninety-nine per cent sure what their response would be, before leaving Newlands Hill.

As they were stopped at the end of the road, in late afternoon, waiting to turn out on to the road to Hesket Newmarket, and then travel on to Carlisle, and eventually Edinburgh, Mr. Thornleigh remarked to his two colleagues, " If we are going to select anybody in Cumberland to do this job for us, it must be that lad. I was impressed by him."

But Eddie didn't know that. Neither did Nora.

Eddie's keen business sense, his only-the-best-will-do pursuit of perfection, his knowledge of the basic slag haulage scene, and the natural place of God in his life had all been evident to the men from I.C.I. But would that be enough to bring the building of a 6,000 ton slag store his way?

And they had all complimented Nora on their dinner. But would her 'boiled tatties' and all the cordial table-talk have influenced the visiting business delegation in any way?

They were only left to wait and wonder.

'Soon, by post', they would know...

17

NOT SO PATIENTLY WAITING

❖

They hadn't long to wait, either. Were spared too much suspense. For within a fortnight a letter arrived. Addressed to Eddie. And there could be no mistaking of its origin for it had I.C.I.'s distinctive company logo embellished on the envelope.

This was the news they had been waiting for.

And it was good. But challenging.

Eddie was being offered the contract to build a basic slag store for I.C.I. However, the firm was obviously anxious to set wheels in motion straight away. They wanted to see the work begun as soon as possible.

The terms of the contract allowed Eddie six weeks in which to decide upon a suitable site on his land, from amongst those they had all considered on the day of their roast-beef-and-Yorkshire-pudding visit. And to obtain planning permission to erect a building on his chosen site.

Then he would have another six weeks to put up the store.

Twelve weeks in all!

Eddie had always loved a challenge. And this was one of his biggest to date.

Daunting, but not insurmountable.

There were three things that Eddie needed to accomplish such a task.

Dedication. Application. And the help and guidance of God.

The first two were qualities that he had possessed from childhood. Whether it had been trapping rabbits, mowing hay, threshing corn or spreading fertiliser on farmers' fields, he had set his own personal performance target. Work as hard as you can for as long as it takes to do the best job possible.

And for the third Nora and he asked God daily in earnest prayer.

It didn't take him long to decide upon the most suitable site. He knew which one the men from I.C.I. had favoured, and agreed with their choice. This was mostly on his own land, just a small piece, for access, having to be acquired from a neighbour, at a reasonable price.

Now that he was sure that he had a large enough site for the mammoth building which he was proposing to erect, Eddie had to obtain planning permission. For this he applied to the County Council offices in Penrith, submitting outline plans.

Then he had to wait. And wait.

It was then that Eddie discovered that there was a fourth quality required in this building business. One in which he recognized himself to be singularly deficient.

Waiting patiently, it was called.

To pass the time profitably until the men in Penrith made up their minds, he decided to use any spare hours he could afford himself, to find out if there were any slag stores of a similar size to the one he was hoping to build, anywhere in the surrounding countryside. The few he knew about were not even half the size of the one he was being expected to erect.

After making a few enquiries from I.C.I. and his basic-slag-in-Middlesbrough contacts, he found that probably the best one for him to visit, the one which would be nearest in storage capacity to his proposed building, was in Wigtown, south west Scotland.

Eddie had already spoken to Roland Hill, a building contractor, and personal friend of his own, about the store building project. And so the two of them set off for Wigtown, Scotland, one summer morning, to see it. They spent the most of a day making a thorough inspection, discussing how various aspects of that existing building could be modified, improved and adapted to suit the Newlands Hill location.

Roland carried a little note-book around with him all day. Then he would say every so often, "Hold on there a minute boy." He had stopped to make yet another weird-to-Eddie sketchy sketch. Just to remind him.

Then when they arrived home Roland used the information in his notebook to draw up a detailed plan of a store to fit on Eddie's site. And satisfy I.C.I's requirements. Complete with elevator and weighbridge.

In mid-July, just as soon as school had finished for the summer vacation, Nora packed up and she and Eddie set out, in their Morris Oxford estate, with four excited children, for a holiday. There were six of them in the car, with all shapes and sizes of boxes of groceries packed into the boot bit. And around their feet. The cases were all strapped onto the roof-rack.

Just by some strange coincidence, too, they were going to stay in a large hired caravan in Sand Green. South west Scotland! The name 'Sand Green' conjured up images of an ideal holiday location. It just had to be a bucket-and-spade kind of place!

One can imagine, then, that the children were not entirely thrilled to discover that the greater part of one of the days of their holiday was to be spent with daddy showing mummy what a **real** slag store looked like!

Throughout those planning days, and the holiday-in-Wigtown week, Eddie had just one reservation about all of this. It was something that would have to be addressed. He believed that God had opened up the way for him to expand his business by giving him the opportunity to build a basic slag store at Newlands Hill. He was busily drawing up plans for a building, and also assessing the carrying capacity of his existing lorries. Even secretly contemplating the possibility of buying another one. Or even two. To enable him to fulfil his undertaking to I.C.I.

But where was the money going to come from for all of this?

Roland had estimated that a slag store of the size that he had planned for Eddie would take somewhere in the region of six thousand pounds to put up.

Then there was the weighbridge which would cost an additional thousand. And the elevator for conveying the slag up into the store. Another thousand.

Total estimated cost of the project, eight thousand pounds!

Now Eddie had worked hard in all his earlier enterprises. And had usually made a profit. But he certainly didn't have that amount of money.

When it comes to the time when payment is required I will always be able to arrange a loan, somehow, he kept assuring himself. There are enough people who know me, and trust me, in business. There must be somebody willing to make me an advance...

That was fair enough.

But there was always an irritating unease at the back of his mind. The what-if-it-doesn't-all-work-out? possibility. It didn't bear contemplation. So he tried hard not to contemplate it.

There was no point in making any approach to anybody yet, though. Not until he was sure that he had planning permission for his store, at least.

On the long-awaited day when the planning committee met in the Council Offices in Penrith, Eddie rang up. It was just after lunch-time. He knew that the meeting had been held in the morning.

And he was incredibly impatient to know the result.

He was straining-at-the-leash. Down-on-the-starting-blocks. Rarin' to go.

When he was informed by someone in the Planning Office that permission had been granted, and that a letter was being sent out to him by post, 'to that effect', Eddie said, "Don't bother to post that letter. I will call in and collect it myself, in person, this afternoon."

He just couldn't wait until the next morning to have that permission in his hand. Anyway, you never know. A letter might just get lost in the post!

As soon as he could possibly shake himself loose from the constraints of that particular day's activity, Eddie drove the twelve miles to Penrith and picked up a brown envelope at the Council Offices. It contained planning permission for him to erect a basic slag store on his land, near Hesket Newmarket.

As he retraced his steps to his car, Eddie's mind was in a pleasant whirl. This was great. This was what he had been hoping, and praying, for, during every day for the past six weeks.

But...

But... now that he had planning permission in his hand, building plans on paper, and buy-more-lorry-plans in his head, where was the money going to come from to set his dream in motion?

That was the next problem...

Suddenly, Eddie's reveries were rapidly interrupted when he realized that the man who was approaching him, smiling, was someone with a far-out family connection. But he was somebody whom Eddie met only rarely. A weddings-and-funerals-and-used-to-send-a-card-at-Christmas type friend.

It was Mr. Norman T. O'Reilly. Accountant.

"Well, look who it is! It's a long time since I have seen you!" was the distant friend's far-from-distant greeting.

Then he went on to enquire, affably, "And tell me, what are you doing with yourself these days, Eddie?"

18

SOME SORT OF AN
ARRANGEMENT

❖

"What am I doing with myself these days?" Eddie echoed the genial enquiry, in almost reflective fashion. As though he was looking back, trying to remember. What was happening, in fact, was that he was battling for thinking time. He had to decide in the next second or two just how much of what he was 'doing these days' his friend would actually want to know.

Was his question merely a form of greeting or was it a genuine enquiry?

It was like asking somebody the common question, "How are you?" There are few things more frustrating than using this question as a form of greeting, only to have it answered. Ten minutes wasted listening to them tell of their indigestion, insomnia, or inabilty to go to work, because of a pain in their back, their neck, or their knee... And that all because you didn't make the simple observation, "Isn't that a better day?"

"Well, actually I am on my way back from the Council offices at the minute," Eddie began, tentatively. "I have just been granted permission to build a basic slag store out at Newlands Hill."

Mr. O' Reilly appeared really interested.

"A slag store. Is that what you are at now? Tell me a bit about it, Eddie. How did you manage to get into that line of work?"

When he realized that his friend's enquiry was more than just a polite greeting, Eddie went on to tell him as much of the story as time spent standing on the street in Penrith would permit.

The start with Harrison Ivinson. The follow-up with Oliver and Snowden. Then I.C.I. And thence to the basic slag store. What could have been a long story had its length dramatically decreased by the docking of detail. Eddie only included enough of the relevant facts to allow his listener to make some sort of sense of what he was 'doing with himself these days.'

Norman O' Reilly was a shrewd man. Used to business affairs and monetary matters. After asking a few peripheral questions about slag, "What kind of stuff is it anyway?" and equipment, "How many lorries and spreaders have you in operation at the minute, Eddie?", he came around to the most fundamental one of all. The issue which he knew that Eddie was going to have to address. The problem that would have to be solved.

Little did he know that the very question he was about to ask had been migrating in and out of Eddie's mind for the previous six weeks.

Now it had come home to roost.

" Forgive me for asking, Eddie, but where is the money going to come from for all of this? Do you have the funds available, or will you need a loan or anything like that?" he enquired, sincerely.

Eddie had to tell the truth. Here was an honest question. And it required an honest answer.

"I have just been thinking about that," he confessed, without divulging just quite how much or for how long. "I know now that I am going to have to make some sort of an arrangement."

Norman T. O' Reilly had listened to the Eddie Stobart story to-date, with a curious concern. An inquisitive interest. Now he regarded his friend with an intent gaze. There was an inexplicable quality of sincerity about this forthright, go-ahead young man that appealed to him.

"Tell me this, Eddie," he had yet another question. "Could you by any chance arrange to put up that slag store by direct labour? It would cut down on labour costs, you know."

"Oh I know that O.K.," Eddie concurred. "Indeed I was planning to do it that way to save money. I have a number of my own men who could help."

He had thought of most things in the previous busy days and weeks.

"Come back with me to my office, Eddie," Mr. O' Reilly invited, suddenly. "I will give you a cheque for two thousand pounds to start you off."

Eddie was flabbergasted.

There he was. Standing on the street in Penrith. Permission to build in a letter in his hand. And a man whom he hadn't seen for a long time was standing in front of him and offering to lend him enough money to 'start him off'!

His, and Nora's prayers, were being answered in a totally unexpected way!

Fifteen minutes later, back in the old-wood-and-furniture polish, bulging-files- and-piles-of-papers atmosphere of Norman O' Reilly's office, they pursued the matter further.

Eddie had been taken aback by both the sudden and sincere nature of his friend's offer. Now it was his turn to make a few enquiries. Clarify the situation.

"What will be the rate of interest on this loan ?" he wanted to know. "And what are the repayment terms?"

"The rate of interest will be 6%," his self-appointed financial consultant informed him, and then with a broad grin went on, "and don't worry about the repayment terms. Yet, anyway. It will be time enough to go into that kind of thing when the job is up and running."

Very appreciative as he was of that kind of consideration, Eddie thought that this man would at least be anxious to see what it was that he was sinking his money in.

"Well, will you come out and see me on the site sometime?" it was his turn to extend an invitation. "Then I can show you the plans and let you see first-hand what it is that I am planning to do."

Mr. O'Reilly was by this time studiously writing a cheque.

He looked up and smiled again.

"Thank you, Eddie, but I don't really need to," he replied. "I know that you know what you are about. I trust you. But when you have worked your way through this," and he proffered Eddie the cheque which he had just completed, "you can come back in here to the office. There will be another two thousand, if you need it, to keep things going until you get into full swing."

Eddie rose to leave the office. His heart and his head were overflowing with a glowing gratitude. He had planned to 'make some sort of an arrangement.'

His heavenly Father, God, had organized the circumstances of that 'arrangement.'

And a far-out-family-friend, Mr. Norman T. O' Reilly, had been charged with taking care of the details.

"It has been nice to see you again, Eddie," the man-he-had-met-on the street said in parting, as they shook hands warmly. "And to be of some help."

Eddie certainly appreciated seeing him. And his help.

By the time he arrived back home to Nora, and Newlands Hill, Eddie had in his possession planning permission for a basic slag store, and a cheque for two thousand pounds to get him started.

He had also a passion to be up and at it straight away!

But that would have to wait another night.

Just 'til the very next morning.

19

TARGET DATE

❖

Next morning Newlands Hill became a hive of activity. Roland Hill arrived to discuss the nature and order of the building operation with Eddie. He was going to erect the steelwork. Two other firms of bricklayers were to be employed to do the brickwork. Eddie undertook to contact them, stressing as usual, his code of practice. Everything had to be done to the highest possible standard. And in this particular case, there was a further proviso. It had to be done in the shortest possible time, as well!

In a few days time large long lorries began to fill the roads from hedge-to-hedge in the Hesket Newmarket area of north Cumberland. They were carrying the first of many steel beams to Newlands Hill.

Stage one of the building was under way.

Just after the first deliveries to the site had been completed and the digging of holes for steelwork and foundations for brickwork had begun, there came a hitch. A snag. The first one. Annoying news.

Eddie heard that the Roads department of the Council had objected to him having been given planning permission to build a slag store on his land. They were concerned that the little quiet country roads around Hesket Newmarket couldn't handle the volume of heavy lorry traffic necessary for the successful operation of such a large store.

This caused him some concern for some days. Always wondering was there some way that the work could be halted. However, since he did have permission in writing he carried on. And was soon assured that it was still in order to do so.

When Roland Hill's men had the steel frame of the building well advanced, the bricklaying squads arrived.

As the work progressed apace, more and more men in more and more little battered vans, seemed to arrive in the yard at Newlands Hill. It was like an invasion. At one stage there were three different contracting firms, responsible for three different aspects of the building, working away. In addition, and depending on the amount of haul-it-and-spread-it work needing be done on any particular day, there were usually three or four of Eddie's own men there too. Labouring. Helping to rocket the building up.

Then there were the four children. Anne, eleven, John, nine, Edward, eight, and nearly-two-year-old toddler William. Each of them was fascinated in his or her own childish way with this huge steel-framed brick-built monster that seemed to be climbing ever closer to the sky. In their own back yard. And they came to like the men who were building it. Ever taunting each other. While banging at something. Or joking with them.

A tremendous sense of camaraderie developed amongst the workmen. Everybody had a target to meet. A goal to achieve. And they all worked hard. There were men up ladders, on scaffolds, at cement mixing machines, or loading yet more stuff from yet another lorry. And they were constantly bantering each other.

One day Roland Hill was up a ladder bolting girders into place. Eddie was informing a small group of the workmen, at ground level, far below, what he considered the next stage in the process to be, as he saw it.

Roland, hearing the conversation, shouted down good-naturedly, "Hey, you down there. Who do you think is the boss here?"

Quick as a flash, one of Eddie's men retorted, "You will find that out when the cheque bounces!"

It was only a joke. And they all knew it.

When the let's-build-a-store-in-six-weeks challenge entered week number four Eddie did what he had been invited to do. He paid a return visit to Mr. Norman T O'Reilly in Penrith. And the man who had been so helpful to Eddie on the first occasion when they met expressed a genuine interest in progress-so-far at Newlands Hill.

He proved to be as good as his word, too, advancing a second two thousand pound loan. This should be sufficient to finish the job, they both reckoned.

After six weeks of frenetic activity, long hours, the occasional minor hitch, and much ribbing and teasing, the basic slag store at Newlands Hill was almost complete. Total cost, four thousand pounds. Two thousand less than the initial estimate. And there had been no short cuts taken, either.

When the last of the contractors pulled out of the yard, they left only one job to be done. It was the concreting of the floor. Eddie had said that he could do that with the help of one or two of his own men. So between arranging for existing orders to be delivered and additional loads to be drawn in to begin filling up the store, Eddie and a few available men laid the floor themselves.

The store was up. Soon the first load of slag arrived. And the new elevator rattled into use...

Eddie had met his deadlines.

And upheld his standards.

Yet another phase of his life had begun.

20

CAN WE COME BACK AGAIN NEXT YEAR?

❖

Although the increasing amount of work with the transportation, storage, and spreading of basic slag occupied Eddie's mind for most of the time on many of the days that summer, it didn't occupy his mind for all of the time on all of the days.

There was another matter which had been causing Nora and him some concern for some time.

It was the need of the neighbourhood.

They knew most of the people who lived in the surrounding countryside. And they knew, too, that most of them didn't know the Saviour who had meant so much to them, for nearly twenty years.

So they commenced a 'cottage meeting' in their home. They invited well-known speakers who were visiting the area, to address this gathering. And very often, when no such talent was available, a local speaker, Mr. Reg Maiden, helped out.

To these meetings, the busy and respected couple invited their friends and neighbours, many of whom were generally pleased to come. Even if they had little interest in what the preacher-man had to say, it was, as they termed it, 'a bit of a night out!' Something different to do.

Then, in the summer of 1964, something happened which was to see these now-and-again type, when-we-can-find-a -suitable-speaker type, meetings, take on a new form. And a much more regular pattern.

Herbert Silverwood, through whose preaching Eddie had become a Christian, had spent the early summer months conducting a mission around the full circuit of all the country Methodist chapels in north Cumberland. A total of twelve in all.

However, as the summer days began to shorten, and summer evenings began to be touched with the chill of approaching autumn, the mission was drawing to its close, and Herbert wanted to mark that close in some sort of a special way. End with a bang. And not with a whimper. He would like to finish the summer of activity by conducting one final get-together for all the churches. A grand closing rally.

Great idea, he thought.

Trouble was, though, that he was the only one who thought that way!

He found himself with a practical problem. An organizational one.

No one single church proved willing to host it for him. Like the men in the Bible who were invited to the big feast, 'they all with one consent began to make excuse'!

They had either too small a building. "Our wee church would never hold a crowd that size!" they said.

Or they were too small a congregation. "We are only a very small number. We could never cater for all the people who would come to the like of that!" they said.

Or they were just too isolated. "We are far too far off the beaten track to hold that kind of a thing. You really need somewhere more central for that!" they said.

And so it went on...

Excuses, excuses, excuses.

This annoyed Eddie.

He hadn't a lot of time for paltry, pathetic, please-don't-ask-US-to-do-anything type petty pretences.

From he was a boy, he had always been used to seeing things through. If he had considered anything to be worth doing, he had wanted to see it done. There and then. And well.

So when he learnt of his friend Herbert Silverwood's vision for one large closing meeting, a grand farewell to summer, he immediately volunteered to host it for him. In a tent. In a neighbour's field.

When Uncle Wilfred, who had been so kind to Eddie in his earlier days, even to the extent of offering him his 'house to let', heard of this plan he was appalled. So much so that he made a point of seeing his nothing's-going-to-stop-me nephew.

"Is it right what I hear, that you are planning to hire a tent and hold a meeting in it?" he enquired, by way of an opener.

"It is. That's right," Eddie replied, not quite sure of what was coming next. "I am."

"Oh, Eddie, you can't do that!" Uncle Wilfred warned, with such sincerity that Eddie began to worry that he was making a grave and mortal mistake. But he couldn't, just on the spur of the moment, think how!

Then the very practical reason for Uncle Wilfred's concern became obvious. "It will cost you far to much!" he continued, in the same terrible-tragedy tone of voice.

"We hired one for our daughter's Janie's wedding, and do you know how much it cost us? You will never guess. Sixty five pound!"

Eddie smiled kindly at his genuinely worried uncle. The uncle who had put himself about to try and stop his go-ahead nephew from going ahead just that single step too far. Over the edge of the ravine, into financial ruin!

"Whatever it costs, Uncle Wilfred, I'm doing it," he maintained firmly, but with feeling. He didn't want to give any offence. "I will be paying for it myself."

"Yourself?" Uncle Wilfred's face was a picture.

"Paying for it yourself," he repeated, with the incredulous air of someone who thought that he hadn't heard properly. "I thought that you would be taking up a collection to cover your expenses. And I was worried in case you would be disappointed if you didn't get enough. Then you could find yourself badly out of pocket."

Eddie then came to realize that his intentions on the matter required some clarification.

"There will be no collection, Uncle Wilfred," he explained. "This is something I want to do for the people of Cumberland. At my expense. God has blessed me, and this is just my simple way of saying 'Thank You'. Of giving something, be it ever so little, back to Him."

"Oh that's different, Eddie!" Uncle Wilfred responded immediately. Puzzled frown gave way to pleasant face in an instant. And concerned uncle became contented uncle, too. Then he pronounced his own personal blessing upon this Eddie-strictly-spiritual-enterprise.

"Go ahead, then. And may God bless your tent meeting. Hope it all works out for you," he concluded. Softly.

Eddie, Nora, and a number of interested and involved Christian friends were praying that it would, as well.

In the days prior to the meeting, Newlands Hill became a hive of activity, again. Many lorries came and went. Most of them were carrying the usual load to the newly-built and becoming-busier slag store. But there were others. They were the only-visiting-vehicles from Murphy's of Rosley. For it was from Murphy's that Eddie had agreed the hire of a two hundred-seater tent. And enough chairs to fill it.

When the carefully-planned-for mid-August Saturday of the meeting finally arrived, it was a fine day. And the people of the district turned up in large numbers for this new event. Over at 'the Stobart place'. And two of the first of the congregation to enter the tent were Uncle Wilfred and his wife, Mabel!

By the time when the service was scheduled to commence, the tent was full. Every seat was taken.

Herbert Silverwood was thrilled to see his vision fulfilled, and he preached the Gospel with a full and thankful heart.

Whether it was the opportunity to catch up with all the local news, Christian or otherwise, over the tea at the end of the meeeting, or the message of the meeting itself, that impressed them, Eddie couldn't quite fathom. There could be no doubting the fact, though, that the people filing and filtering reluctantly out and away, had been impressed. By something.

By far the most common reaction of those leaving was a comment with a question. "That was a great afternoon, Eddie. We really enjoyed that! Will you be doing something like it again, next year?"

Whilst appreciating their encouraging remarks, Eddie wasn't very sure, at that particular moment, what he was going to be doing, 'next year'. He was only too glad to see that particular day over successfully.

Anyway, he wasn't certain that he wanted to stage some sort of a pleasant Saturday afternoon's entertainment for the local church-goers. Something for Christians to 'enjoy'. That wasn't the aim of the exercise.

Though perhaps important in itself. His and Nora's purpose in arranging such a meeting had been to see their friends and neighbours come to a personal knowledge of Jesus Christ.

So his answer to the oft-repeated enquiry, "Can we come again next year?" was suitably noncommittal.

"We will consider next year, next year," he invariably replied, adding with a grin, "and we promise to let you know what conclusion we come to. Next year!"

21

A FLEECE BEFORE THE LORD

❖

Following upon the apparent popularity of that August afternoon with the local people, Eddie and Nora had a question to answer. A problem to solve.

Would they hold a similar meeting next year? Or not?

Throughout the busy autumn months, and on into the shorter days and longer nights of winter, they gave the matter much careful consideration.

Nora was still busy transporting workmen from place to place, from field to field, in the van. And looking after the children. Eddie had few spare moments, either. For the volume of work just seemed to increase by the month.

Early in 1965, and since there was always the possibility that there would be another such meeting in the summer, Eddie bought the 'tent field' from his neighbour.

At least now they were prepared. Should God lead them to organize a second summer rally.

With spring came the snowdrops, the crocuses and the daffodils. And a renewed volley of questions from all quarters.

"What about the summer meeting in the tent, Eddie? You said you would have made a decision about that next year."

There was no escaping it.

Something had to be done. Or said.

Eddie and Nora prayed for guidance. And came to a considered conclusion.

Provided they could find a suitable and willing speaker, they would arrange a Bible-teaching weekend in August, with two separate meetings. They would serve tea for all late on Saturday afternoon, with an evening meeting to follow. Then a final gathering on the Sunday evening.

Having committed themselves to going ahead for that year at least, then they pleaded for a sign from the Lord. Was this to be the last of the summer rallies? The second of two. Or was it to be the second of a series that would run on and on?

What they asked of the Lord was that He would grant them a definite sign. They prayed earnestly that if they were to continue these meetings on an annual basis, God would bring some one to Himself in that particular summer. Then they would know. For sure.

Now that they had put out their 'fleece before the Lord', and had decided, provisionally, to have a weekend of meetings, they needed to have an acceptable speaker booked, before any final arrangements could be made.

Nora suggested Stan Ford. Since she had been saved under his preaching, Eddie and she had kept in regular contact with the big burly former-boxer.

When approached, Stan expressed himself delighted to come.

Now everything was in order.

When the Saturday of the first meeting arrived, so did the crowds. All the people who had been asking for it had obviously been looking forward to it. And they must have brought their friends as well. For the tent was full. Packed. For the second year running.

A pair of Eddie and Nora's friends, James and Madge Tweddle, started a new trend, too. They brought their caravan with them and parked it in the tent field. Right beside the tent. To be as close as they could to the action!

Crowd enthusiasm, popular demand and a big attendance were not sufficient to satisfy Eddie and Nora, as to their sign from the Lord, though.

Successful football teams had all those things, they knew. They needed something more.

Something different.

Something special.

Something spiritual.

As that Saturday progressed, however, two things did happen which were significant. Special. And spiritual.

One of those results of the day at Newlands Hill though totally unexpected, was to prove expansive and fruitful. The other outcome, which could, and perhaps, should, have been expected since it had been prayed for, but everybody was far too busy to believe could **really** happen, was local, personal and exciting.

The first positive product of that Saturday came during the chatting over tea, late in the afternoon. It was then that Mr. Williamson, who was at that time Chief Constable of Northampton, and visiting relatives in Cumberland, moved around speaking to a number of influential Christian men whom he knew. Men who had come for the Bible teaching. And to meet friends from other Christian groups.

Mr. Williamson had 'done his homework'. And chosen his contacts carefully. He had a specific reason for talking to each of these particular men. His wasn't just a great-to-see-you! well-how-are-you? type of conversation. The kind of chit-chat men engage in with their long-lost friends whilst trying to avoid blistering their tongue on straight-from-the-boiler-tea, and simultaneously preventing their apple-cream from cracking and crumbling and crawling creamily down their tie.

No. He had a purpose in mind. This was a field ripe and ready for harvesting, as far as he was concerned. A place to give his vision heads and hearts.

Chief Constable Williamson was anxious to see a branch of The Gideons established in Cumberland. And here were some ideal men to set it in motion. A wonderful nucleus with which to commence such a work.

He approached each man in turn, individually, with the proposition. Each proved agreeable. Enthusiastic, even.

So a local Gideon branch was formed, to distribute copies of the Bible and New Testament into schools, hospitals, hotels and prisons in the district. Wherever people passed through, they would make the Scriptures available. For help, consolation, and comfort.

A reassuring, but totally unforseen, result of the day's activity.

It was great, but was it all?

Eddie was pleased to be a part of it, but could there be something more to come?

What had God still in store for them?

It wasn't until after the evening meeting that Eddie and Nora received a definitive answer to their query. Do we go on, or not?

Mr. Reg Maiden, a Christian friend of the Stobart family, led the evening session. In the early introductory time, Reg, who was a talented singer, invited James Tweddle to join him in the singing of a duet. When James agreed, rather shyly, he joined his friend on the platform.

And they sang.

The singing was powerful and tuneful. But tender and touching, too.

It set the atmosphere for the remainder of the evening.

Stan Ford, when his time came to preach, did so with obvious conviction. It was clear to all present that he believed what he was talking about. It was very real to him, and he appeared intent upon making it real to everyone else.

At the close of that service people were moved. Touched by the power and presence of God. Stan Ford asked anyone who would like to come to know the Saviour, to raise their hand.

Then Reg Maiden asked those people who had indicated that they would like to hear more, to go over into the house at Newlands Hill. Where they could speak to someone, 'in private'. He also appealed for counsellors to accompany them.

Later, when most of the crowds, who had declared themselves 'blessed', had gone back to their cars, or set off on foot for home, Eddie and Nora went back over, happily, wearily, to their own house.

And what a sight met them there!

Looking in through the living-room window, as they passed, they saw two people, deep in conversation. Somebody was counselling somebody.

The somebody being counselled was young, they noticed.

It was a girl.

Indeed it was none other than their own daughter, Anne!

A few minutes later, Anne, aged nearly thirteen, came out to greet them, her whole countenance aglow.

"I came out to tell you, mummy and daddy," she began, her face a wonderful expression of exuberant joy. She was beaming broadly, and yet the tears were at the bubbling up and just-about-to-overflow-down-her-cheeks stage.

"I have got saved!" she exclaimed, throwing her arms around both of them in turn.

Nora and Eddie were absolutely thrilled.

Two of their most fervent prayers had been answered. In the same event and instant. Anne, whom they had prayed for since before she was born, had come to know Jesus Christ as her Saviour.

And God had provided them with their 'sure sign', as well.

He had moved right in on their family and called their eldest child to Himself!

What could be clearer than that?

The summer weekend in the tent in the field was set to become an annual event.

From that day forward!

22

WHAT WILL WE DO ON SUNDAY MORNING?

❖

Fully convinced that God had indicated clearly to them that the August weekend of Bible teaching was a worthwhile exercise, Eddie and Nora arranged a similar weekend for the next year. 1966.

They decided to increase the number of meetings, yet again. This time to cover the whole weekend. One on Friday night. Another on Saturday after tea in the afternoon. And the final closing rally on the Sunday evening.

Mr. John Robb, from Glasgow, was the invited speaker.

As they had done in the two previous years, so the people came again to the third weekend. In large numbers. And the idea of bringing the family caravan along seemed to have taken on also. People came towing their touring caravans which they parked in one of the many sites in the area. These were interested Christians who had heard of the weekend from others, and didn't want to miss a single word!

During the tea interval on the Saturday afternoon., John Robb approached the owner of Newlands Hill. Slag-haulier, fertilizer-spreader, weekend-organizer.

"What are we doing tomorrow morning, Eddie?" he enquired.

"What do you mean, what are we doing tomorrow morning?" Eddie, momentarily taken aback, answered a question with a question. Then he added, gathering that the speaker was trying to find out about morning worship, "Just going to the local churches, probably."

"Then why not have a Communion service for all of us? Here. In the tent," he suggested.

"Yes. That sounds like a good idea," Eddie agreed.

After he had spoken to a few others whom he thought would be keen to be involved, Eddie told Mr. Robb to announce a Communion service for all interested Christians. Next morning, in the tent.

Eddie and Nora had made diligent preparations for that weekend. They had planned for everything. And for everybody. As well as they could, and as far as was possible. For, if 'only the best will do' in everyday, workaday matters, then they considered it vitally important that this policy should also apply to a Christian-fellowship-Gospel-outreach weekend.

Outdoor event organizers have discovered, since the days of Noah's ark, however, that there is one element over which they have no control. The weather.

Eddie and Nora were no exception to this rule.

It had been raining steadily all that Saturday, and by the time the evening meeting came the field around the tent was an absolute quagmire. A swamp.

Those brave souls, whose job it had been to serve the tea, had squelched and splashed around the entrance until the tent door looked as though it had been ploughed by oxen in a thunderstorm. A mess.

Just after John Robb had led the congregation in the opening praise, and announced the Communion service next morning, the rain became heavier. It drummed with a hollow monotony on the layer of taut canvas that covered the congregation. The tent roof.

Mr. Robb chose, as his text for that meeting, 'How shall we escape, if we neglect so great salvation?' (Hebrews 2 v.3) He preached with conviction. Genuine sincerity. Trying valiantly to make himself heard above the persistent rhythm of the rain on the roof.

By then the saturated ground in the field outside had refused to absorb any more water. So little rivulets began to enter the tent. A mere trickle at first. And some people smiled to see the water carve out a course for itself amongst handbags and folded-on-the-floor raincoats.

Soon though, the rivulets grew in both volume and speed. They flowed in the top end of the tent. And out the bottom. Swelling the sawdust floor into a sticky paste.Bending over the unsawdusted grass.

John Robb preached away. He was dry enough, up on the platform!

People sat listening as best they could. Some had to move their feet to one side to allow the floodwater through. Others were forced to lift them up and hold them up, for there was nowhere to put them down.

The children saw the funny side of it all. They did all sorts of contortions to watch the water. In front of them. Below their seats. Gushing out again at the back. It was also some fun to watch well-dressed ladies in well-priced clothes trying to save their Sunday best!

But the severe weather also brought with it a sense of awe. Of darkness during daylight. Almost of doom. And the words, 'How shall we escape...?' echoing around the tent seemed chillingly appropriate, somehow.

The presence of God was experienced that evening in a most unusual way. And the blessing of God ensued.

Eddie's two sisters, Dorothy and Isobel, both trusted in Christ for salvation, and so too did some young people.

It was a night that many people remembered, and talked about for months to come. For a variety of different reasons.

Next morning, Sunday, they met in the tent for a Communion service. Some called it a 'Breaking-of-Bread' meeting. The attendance, though was nothing like what it had been the night before. Or what it would be later on that day. For most of the previous evening's congregation were involved in their own churches across Cumberland, and beyond.

Despite the relatively small number, however, there was a real sense of praise to God for his goodness, and thanks to the Saviour for His love, in that service.

It made such a lasting impression on those present, in fact, that Eddie and Nora volunteered to hold such a meeting every Sunday morning for interested local Christians. In their home.

As with the business, so with the Sunday morning service. From humble beginnings it was destined to develop into something much bigger.

For the next two years, every Sunday morning, a Communion service was held in Newland Hill, with ten or twelve attending.

Then, when others who had heard about the meeting appeared drawn to join them, Eddie realized that the time had come to consider expansion. And the establishment of something much more permanent.

But where were they to go?

It seemed like an answer to prayer then, when in 1968, he heard that Union Street Hall in nearby Wigton was up for sale. When he first went to have a look at it, though, what Eddie saw filled him with hope, and despair. All at once.

The hall was a reasonable size. It would be very suitable for their purpose. Another plus point about it was that it was central to the district, so many of the regular attenders would find it easier to travel to than Newlands Hill. And by far the greatest factor of all in its favour was that it was in the heart of their local market town.

In Wigton they could become more than just a Sunday morning worshipping group. They could also become an actively outwardly witnessing group. Presenting the Gospel to the people of the town and district.

The downside of the proposed purchase was the state of the place. It was in very poor condition. A shambles. Hadn't seen the head of a hammer or the hair of a paintbrush for years.

Eddie knew, though, that willing hands could always effect essential repairs. So he bought the property. At an if-you-really-want-it-you-can-have-it price.

The group then set to work with a will, doing what they could to make the building basically useable. And when the immediate clearing and repair work had been done, the Sunday morning in Newlands Hill group moved base, and became the Union Street Hall in Wigton group.

After some months in that Hall, and observing a growing interest amongst Christians in the local community in the gathering, Eddie realized that two things needed to be done, to establish the new 'church', for that is what it was, on a more permanent basis.

Their building needed a major refurbishment, if it was to become their regular place of worship. And a group of trustees would have to be set up to administer the church affairs.

So, when he had discussed these matters with others they began work again. This time it wasn't merely a superficial clean-and-dust-to-we-see-how-it-goes job. It was a major pull down and throw out, then replace and repaint operation.

While the actual building in which the members were to meet was being refurbished,the trustees were being appointed.

Those who helped and advised Eddie in the founding of that church were eager that it should be established on evangelical Christian principles. So they defined the qualifications of a trustee in unmistakeable yet understandable language.

A trustee of that church had to be someone who had 'accepted Jesus Christ as his own and personal Saviour and recognised the Bible to be God's infallible Word'.

A sound foundation.

And the church grew.

For they recognised that their new location brought with it new responsibilities to the people of Wigton. New opportunities for outreach.

Those responsibilities they were willing to undertake.

Those opportunities they were prepared to seize.

23

SHARES OR SHEEP?

❖

Meanwhile the business was bounding on. Going from strength to strength. The lorries seemed to be always roaring along the roads of Cumberland. Either loaded going to deliver, or unladen going to collect. A steady stream of them visited the massive store at Newlands Hill, daily. The men with the spreaders were kept steadily employed, too. Working hard from early morning until late in the evening, especially in the spring.

In July, 1968, daughter Anne left school and commenced work in the office in the yard. This move was necessary, and welcome, for two reasons. The first was the increase in business which had brought with it an unavoidable increase in administration and paper work. The second reason was more pressing. And potentially more serious.

Nora, who had been ever-involved in the day-to-day running of the business, right from the early always-leave-the-stackyard-tidy threshing mill days, and was now involved in the ferrying-men-from-farm-to-farm-in-the-van operation, as well as attending to the office work, became ill. She had been unwell for quite some time and had been in hospital on a number of occasions.

Her illness, plus the responsibility of a growing family, had meant that she was unable to help out as once she did.

So the fact that Anne didn't have to return to school in September, since she would by then be sixteen years of age, came as a great relief to her then-ailing mum.

And still the business boomed.

A new trailer truck was purchased to help out with the increased demand for fertiliser. To augment the already ageing fleet.

The year end for the Eddie Stobart collect it, store-it, sell-it or spread-it business was May 31st, each year.

In the early summer of 1970, Eddie studied the figures for the previous year's trading carefully. To assess, in detail, the business year past. June 1969 - May 1970.

Having considered the situation carefully he discovered a couple of interesting things. These, in turn, spurred him into further action.

The first fact was that the accountant had allowed for the normal depreciation of the lorries which he was operating. When Eddie looked at the paper valuation of each lorry he realized that because of the type of the lorries, and the nature of the work, some of them were not worth their balance sheet value.

In addition to that, he was encouraged to find that the year's trading had made an overall profit of some nine thousand pounds. He was thoroughly discouraged, on the other hand, to realize that this amount was liable to a substantial tax payment.

There was only one way in which he deal with this situation, in a legal business sense, he was advised. And that was to form a limited company. He could then arrange to have all the lorries valued, and accounted for at their true valuation.

After studying all the implications of this matter very carefully from every aspect, and listening to lots of well-intentioned advice, Eddie decided to pursue this course of action.

So it was that on 1st November, 1970, a new company was formed. It was called simply, Eddie Stobart Ltd., and the share value of the company was ten thousand pounds, fully paid.

The newly-established company had two directors. Eddie Stobart, who held nine thousand of the shares, and his daughter, Anne Stobart, who was by then over eighteen years of age. She held the remaining one thousand shares.

The company of Eddie Stobart Ltd. then carried on its operations. Successfully.

Not wishing, ever, to make any difference in their family, Eddie and Nora were anxious to make sure that all of their children were afforded an equal opportunity to become shareholders in the not-long-going but already-expanding company. They were soon to discover, though, as parents have been doing all down the centuries, that all of the members of a family do not have the same interests. There are individual differences.

When son John became eighteen, in October, 1971, he too was offered, like big sister Anne, one thousand shares in the company. John, however, wasn't all that interested in either driving lorries or spreading slag. And he certainly had no aspirations to spend his life working in an office! He had a compelling ambition. An attraction in another direction.

Ever since boyhood he had been interested in farming. And farm animals, particularly. The raising of livestock. Like his grandfather, the John Stobart after whom he had been called, he wanted to work on the land. With animals. Be a farmer.

So he asked for, and was given, his shares in cash.

One thousand pounds.

To buy sheep.

24

TRY ASKING ME

❖

In the autumn of 1969, Eddie's father, John, asked his son if he would be interested in hearing a really good speaker. Eddie and Nora were always interested in hearing 'really good speakers', for they were constantly on the lookout for someone new to come and address their by then well-established and eagerly-anticipated August Bible teaching weekend.

"Yes, I would indeed like to hear a 'good speaker' as you say," he replied. "Who is it?"

"I believe Dr. Martyn Lloyd-Jones is speaking at special services in High Bentham this week. Perhaps we could go down and hear him some night." Father's item of information also included a thinly veiled suggestion. It was clear that he would be anxious to go and hear the man himself, but would be unable to drive so far on his own.

Eddie and Nora agreed to take his father and Ruth, to hear this man, this 'good speaker', whom he knew very little about, some night. So a date was arranged.

On the way down from Hesket Newmarket to High Bentham in North Yorkshire, Eddie and Nora wondered to themselves if anybody was worth coming this distance to hear. The road seemed to wind endlessly on and on.

However, since father appeared unusually eager, almost to the point of subdued excitement to hear this preacher he had told them about, they thought that their trip would probably turnout to be worthwhile. It would certainly pass all of the evening and part of the night for them, anyway, driving to High Bentham and back!

When the gracious elderly gentleman began to speak, though, they realized that there was something different, unique, almost, about this Bible teacher. There was such a quality of Christian radiance about his personality and such a profound depth of thought presented in plain uncomplicated language, about his preaching. And these two wonderfully complementary characteristics combined to make that meeting something very special.

John Stobart, whose idea it had been to come in the first place, his wife Ruth, son Eddie and daughter-in-law Nora, sat spellbound, with dozens of others, listening to the man. Hanging upon his every word.

Now at that moment in time Eddie didn't know a lot about Dr. Martyn Lloyd- Jones. And he had never heard of Westminster Chapel. He may have heard well-informed city-type Christians mention his name at one time or another. And he seemed to recall having seen the name on or in a book somewhere. He couldn't remember where, or when, though. For he didn't, at that time, go in a lot for books. To him, two hours spent sitting reading a book would constitute a serious waste of time. After all, you could be halfway to Middlesbrough with a trailer truck, or have a really big field half-spread with fertiliser in that length of time!

When he saw the man, and heard him expound the Scriptures that evening, however, he was attracted to him straightaway.

Turning to Nora when the service was over, and the large crowd had begun to shuffle slowly out into the October night, he said, emphatically, "I'm going to ask that man if he would come and speak at our weekend next August."

So they waited. And waited. And waited.

They wanted to have time to introduce themselves to Dr. Lloyd-Jones, tell him something about the August weekend, and give him a proper invitation. But by the number of people who were queueing up quietly to speak to him they came to the conclusion that at least fifty per cent of Yorkshire had decided to do something the same!

Eventually it came their turn.

Eddie introduced Nora, Ruth, his father and himself to the patient gentleman, who seemed to have time to spend with everybody who spoke to him. Then, after expressing how much they had been blessed by the service, he paved the way for the invitation to come, by asking, "Why have you never preached in Cumberland?"

Dr. Martyn Lloyd-Jones raised his eyebrows. It was a natural reaction of puzzled surprise. Affording the matter no more than a mere split second's thought he replied with a mischievous smile, "Probably because I have never been asked!"

All five of them laughed. That was a sound enough reason for not going somewhere, they would all be willing to concede.

When the brief burst of laughter had subsided, Eddie pursued the subject. "Well, would you come if you were asked?" he persisted. "For I am asking you now. We hold a Bible teaching weekend in a tent beside our home in August each year. And we would be really delighted if you could come and help us with that."

"I don't have my next year's diary with me here," the highly revered Bible scholar explained, in response to the come-up-to-Cumberland-and-help-us invitation, "but if you write to me at home, with your dates, I promise you I will consider it. And come if I possibly can."

After giving Eddie his address, Dr. Lloyd-Jones excused himself and went across to speak to someone else who had remained resignedly in the porch. Waiting for him. And Eddie, Nora, John and Ruth set off. Back up the A6. To Hesket Newmarket.

Keen to have such a man for the August weekend in the following year, Eddie and Nora wrote to Dr. Martyn Lloyd-Jones very soon after returning home. And in less than a fortnight they received his reply.

No, it said. He couldn't come in August as he was fully committed for that month. But he would be free to come at the end of May. For the Bank Holiday weekend. Would that be suitable? Or did it have to be August?

Unwilling to let such an opportunity pass unseized-upon, the weekend organizers replied almost at once, informing Dr. Lloyd-Jones that the weekend he had suggested would be fine. And thus it was arranged.

When May, 1970, came, Eddie drove up to collect the much-in-demand speaker and his wife from Gatehouse-of-Fleet, in Scotland, where they had been staying for a short holiday.

On the Friday evening, the first evening of the weekend series, Eddie and Nora were amazed to see the cars begin to arrive and park around Newlands Hill shortly after 6.30 p.m. The meeting, they were sure, had been advertised to begin at 7.30!

When the 7.30 starting time did come around the tent was packed. The family ended up helping to carry chairs across from the house into the tent . To help seat the people. And by the time Dr. Martyn Lloyd-Jones rose to speak there were people sitting in every available space. On a weird assortment of forms and chairs. And some of the 'helpers', who were unable to find anything suitable to sit upon, ended up standing around the door.

Later that evening, and on the next day, the Saturday, Eddie and Nora discovered that increasing numbers of the congregation had come to Cumberland with their caravans. And had parked on surrounding sites. James and Madge Tweddle's idea of five years before had certainly caught on, and taken off. And the local caravan site owners didn't object, apparently!

That weekend proved to be the beginning of many wonderful weekends for the Stobarts.

The meetings were great. The teaching was both profound, and practical. And the people flocked to them from all parts. Coming as early as they could to procure a seat within sight and sound of the speaker. And staying as long as they could. To learn all they could, both from, and about, the man.

Something even more enduring happened, too.

When Dr. Lloyd-Jones and his wife were leaving for home on Tuesday morning, having promised to 'come back again next year', for the meetings, Eddie and Nora realized that they had benefitted personally, as well as spiritually from that particular weekend experience.

For they had made two new, lifelong friends.

25

THE SAME, ONLY DIFFERENT

❖

In the late summer of 1972, and after repeated applications, Eddie Stobart became an agricultural merchant, in his own right. No need for the help of firms like Harrison Ivinson, Oliver and Snowden, or even I.C.I., now. He could trade in agricultural supplies where and when he wished.

Having been granted an agricultural merchant's licence, Eddie wasn't long until he started to make full use of it. While continuing to sell, and spread, fertilizer from Newlands Hill, as he had always done, he recognised another potentially profitable proposition. Why expect farmers to come to him when he could increase his stock, widen his scope, and sell them agricultural hardware where they were? Where they congregated. With money in their pockets to meet the needs on their farms.

So he began selling farm supplies from a caravan in Wigton market every Tuesday. Market day.

This venture proved so popular that it wasn't long until Eddie was looking for somewhere bigger in the Wigton area. Somewhere more permanent. His customers were beginning to ask him if he could obtain and stock a much wider variety of agricultural requisites. Items which Eddie soon realized that were essential to the farming community, but hadn't been part of his initial stock list. There were other things, too, larger spare parts for farm machinery, for example, and the problem with them was the space. You just couldn't keep them in your Tuesday-in-the-market caravan. That is if you wanted to get into it yourself!

In November of that same year, Eddie became aware that a 'For Sale' notice had gone up on an almost derelict property in the town centre. Nobody had occupied that shop for years. Story was, amongst the locals, that some nameless, faceless, not-from-the-district, well-to-do individual had purchased it years ago for his daughter. She was supposed to be going to start up a boutique, they said.

Nothing ever happened, though. The boutique never materialised.

Thus the property had been left untended for years.

The exterior paintwork was faded and flaking. The windows were boarded up.

And the stale-smelling cobweb-covered interior had become home and playground to all manner of flying and humming, creeping and crawling, spinning and scuttling things. A mecca for minibeasts.

Many seasons had come and gone without the happy ring of a human laugh or echoing thump of a hurrrying footstep ever shattering the silence of their sanctuary.

Having viewed it from the outside, it didn't take Eddie long to appreciate its possibilities, though.

It was central.

It was big. Much bigger than a caravan. And too big for a boutique, really.

It backed out on to a car park, which would be handy for loading and unloading.

If it could be bought at a reasonable price he reckoned that, like the Union Street Hall, it would be a worthwhile acquisition. A few months spent repairing, replacing, replumbing, replastering and repainting would transform it into a viable shop.

Who owned it, though? And could he negotiate a satifactory purchase?

On making enquiries, Eddie was informed that the shambles had been put up for sale by a trawler owner. A Mr. Thomsen. A Norwegian, with a fishing fleet based in Whitehaven.

He was anxious to find out more about the property, including the conditions of sale, since it could easily be adapted to suit his requirements. So Eddie contacted Mr. Thomsen, through an agent, and made an appointment to see him.

On arriving at Mr. Thomsen's premises in Whitehaven, Eddie was somewhat surprised to be subjected to rigorous security checks. He was asked to give proof of his identity, and was then plied with a series of questions as to why he was there.

After some time of waiting around, the prospective buyer was escorted to Mr. Thomsen's office. Where the questioning began all over again! Before that trawler owner was going to sell anything to anybody he was going to attempt to ensure that everything was in order. Sensible business practice, no doubt.

Eddie didn't mind. He was in no hurry. Neither English Heritage nor The National Trust were exactly clamouring to buy the place the man had for sale. Nor, it seemed, was anybody else.

So Eddie took his time. Told Mr. Thomsen about the threshing. The slag and the slag-store building. The number of lorries he had on the road. He finished up by explaining that he was now an agricultural merchant looking for a base from which to expand his agricultural merchandising. And opening a shop in Wigton was an idea that had occurred to him.

Having heard the Eddie Stobart story to date, the hitherto tense Mr. Thomsen seemed to relax a little. Settling back into his armchair behind a massive desk, he told Eddie something of his story. How he had come from Norway to Britain and had bought a fishing trawler. "Now I have a fleet of them", he said, unpretentiously.

As he was talking, Eddie was having a leisurely look around him. If this man wasn't busy telling me that he was a trawler fleet owner, he mused inwardly, I could probably have guessed it for myself. From this office.

For the walls were all adorned with down-to-the-sea-in-ships reminders. There were paintings of trawlers battling their way through monstrous waves. In stark contrast to them, there was also a written-over calendar sporting a picture of fishing boats in a sunny harbour. All very pleasant. Not even a sign of the smell. And right behind Mr. Thomsen himself was a picture of a big, ugly-looking fish with its mouth gaping open. It seemed as though it was about to bite the man's head off.

There's no accounting for taste, thought Eddie.

When they eventually got around to the business of the day, it was all relatively simple. Judging from the level of security that Mr. Thomsen lived behind, and some of the facts which he had merely hinted at during his getting-to-know you introductory discourse, Eddie gathered that this prominent businessman had his own personal pile of problems to deal with. So he would probably welcome the opportunity to rid himself of the wreck in Wigton. It would always be one more problem less.

After they had agreed the purchase price of three thousand five hundred pounds, they signed and settled. As they shook hands on the deal the doubts began to flood into Eddie's mind. He had just begun to ask himself, 'Am I daft or what?', when he noticed that Mr. Thomsen was smiling. It was a kind of an I-don't-do-this-often-but-I-have-to-do-it-sometime fleeting flickering smile. The fact that he was three and a half thousand pounds better off, and a useless-to-him property less, no doubt helped.

"Glad to meet you, Mr. Stobart. We have both had very similar business experiences," he remarked.

Eddie held the hand that was shaking his for an extra moment or two, as he looked into Mr. Thomsen's eyes. They were by now standing, regarding each other across the shiny, solid desk. There was something about the pathetic isolation of the trawler tycoon in his position of power that struck a chord in his heart. Alerted him to a spiritual need.

"I suppose you could say that in many ways we are the same," he conceded. "But I must admit that I can see that there are at least two ways in which you and I are different."

"And what are those?" Mr. Thomsen enquired with a puzzled look, unused to having people disagree with him. Releasing his hand from the holding handshake he leant forward on the tops of eight fingers and two thumbs, spread out on the desk.

"Well, for one thing your business track record is far more impressive than mine," Eddie proceeded to explain. He had been invited to furnish further information, and that he would be only too glad to do.

"But there is another difference between us also," he continued.

"It is a personal one. You see, when I was seventeen years of age I trusted Jesus Christ as my Saviour. I became a Christian. And I doubt if you ever did that."

Eddie could tell by the wave of recognition which crossed the trawler owner's face that he knew exactly what he was talking about.

Mr. Thomsen sank back into his chair.

A short silence followed.

When he finally did reply it was clear that Eddie's words had shot straight to the core of his innermost being. Had penetrated the security cordon which he had thrown up around his soul.

"I should have been a Christian , too," he blurted out at length. "My parents were both Christians and I was brought up in that sort of a home. But during the war I lost all interest in Christian things. To tell you the truth I even doubt sometimes if there is a God at all, now. I have turned my back on all my parents believed. And taught me so faithfully."

There was a second short pause, and then Mr. Thomsen concluded his confession with a sigh, and the statement, "And I'm sure there is no hope for me now."

Surprised though he was at this wealthy but sad and insecure man's open expression of his most secret feelings, Eddie had his answer ready.

"Of course there is hope for you still, " he responded reassuringly. "As long as we have breath in our lungs we can still make our peace with God. That is what happened to one of the thieves on the cross. Right in his dying minutes. Now is your opportunity to get right with God. Your parents have often told you, I'm sure, about the love of God, and the death of Christ for your sins. Why don't you come to Him? Now. Here. Today. He is still calling you. Still expecting you. Trust Him."

Recognizing that he had said enough, and would have to leave the matter between Mr. Thomsen and the God whose very existence he had even begun to question, Eddie turned to leave.

"Thank you very much for everything, Mr. Stobart," the man behind the desk said, rising and holding out his hand yet again. "Hope the shop works out well for you."

"Thank you, Mr. Thomsen. Thank you," Eddie replied, and left.

As he walked back across the car park to his car, a few minutes later, Eddie wondered about that man. With every early opportunity, with more money than he could ever spend, sealed in his own self-imposed isolation. And with the God of his parents shut out of his heart and life.

He then reflected on the chance he had been given to challenge him with the claims of Christ. Very few people were ever going to be permitted to approach that prosperous but lonesome, security-conscious businessman.

"Thank You, God, for allowing me to speak to Mr. Thomsen. Save him, Lord. Save him," he prayed, earnestly.

Repeatedly.

26

WOULD YOU HAVE A LORRY THERE?

❖

Many of the local Wigton people were amazed to see the work men move in over the winter to the shop which they were convinced they would never see open for business again. It was such a ramshackle. Had been empty for so long.

January and February of 1973 saw a steady procession of workmen, builders, joiners, plumbers, plasterers, electricians and painters reduce the property to an empty echoing shell. Then bit by bit, blow by blow, brush-stroke by brush-stroke, they put it all back together again. When at last they had finished ferrying away lorry loads of rubbish, Eddie began. Ferrying in lorry loads of agricultural and garden supplies.

The curiosity of many of the townsfolk was satisfied when, in late February, a newly painted signboard appeared above the newly shined shop window. It informed them that these new business premises were to be a Farm, Home and Garden Shop. The smaller print in the brackets below let them know, too, who the owner, the new agricultural merchant, was. Eddie Stobart Ltd..

1st March, 1973, was a big day for Eddie and Nora, for it was on that day that their new shop opened in Wigton. And it was also on that day that their first grandchild, Fiona, was born, to Anne and her husband, Ken.

Some excitement! Nora spent the day in a kind of a whirl. Not quite sure where to be. Or what to do, first.

Early spring was an ideal time to open a farm, home and garden shop. It suited farmers and gardeners alike. Their busy season. And the home people, the housewives? Well, any season suited them. The needs of the home were ever ongoing, they would all agree.

This new venture proved to be popular with the local community. A service which they needed, and which they were therefore happy to support. All through the summer Eddie was encouraged by the increase in business, as more and more people from the outlying districts heard about 'the new shop in Wigton'.

The fertilizer business was going well, too. The lorries and spreaders were kept constantly on the move.

Then, as happens so often in the life of all of us, and it had happened in the life of Eddie and Nora before, when things appear to be rolling along just fine, everything slithers to a sudden and shattering halt.

Something totally unexpected occurs...

In October, 1973, Eddie and Nora decided to have a few days break, away from the regular day-to-day humdrum round of activity. So they travelled up to Largs on the Ayrshire coast, for a short holiday. For the period of their absence, their daughter Anne, with Ken and baby Fiona, took up temporary residence in Newlands Hill. So that Anne could 'look after the boys'. 'The boys' who were fast becoming men. John as by that time twenty. Edward was eighteen. Indeed William, who was nearly twelve, was really the only 'boy'.

Both Eddie and his wife were happy with the arrangement though. For Nora had every confidence in her daughter Anne's ability to look after her younger brothers.

Just as she would have done herself.

Eddie, also, had every confidence in his daughter Anne's ability to take care of the running of the business.

Just as he would have done himself.

So it was Anne who sustained the initial shock. Opened the letter containing the unwelcome news.

Loath as she was to interrupt her parent's holiday, for 'they needed a break' she reckoned, yet this news had to be passed on immediately. It was too weighty for her young-mother, big-sister, office-manager shoulders to carry alone. She would have to let them know.

On Monday morning, the phone rang in Eddie and Nora's Largs hotel.

"A call for you, Mr. Stobart", the receptionist said.

It was Anne. Anxious to share the burden.

"Dad, there is a letter here in the post this morning from Fisons," she began, struggling to keep her composure. "It is to let us know that they have taken over all of I.C.I.'s agricultural outlets, including basic slag. Then it goes on to say that they won't be needing our slag store any more. They are giving us one month's notice. Then they are pulling out..."

Anne was annoyed. Understandably so.

It was disappointing, verging upon distressing, news. For the collection, storage and spreading of basic slag had become the backbone of the business. Other interests were merely profitable sidelines by comparison. For Eddie Stobart Ltd. to lose it would be like having your luxury liner sink below you, leaving you to spend the rest of your life jumping to and fro amongst the lifeboats.

Eddie, daddy, was having a great holiday, though.

And he had a great God. So he could afford to be positive, even though all the warning lights had suddenly come on in his business brain. As they had done on a number of previous occasions.

"Don't worry about it, Anne," he reassured his daughter. "Your mum and I will be home on Wednesday, and between us we will sort something out."

Despite his encouraging words to Anne, Eddie spent two more not entirely carefree days on his holiday. He and Nora talked through the implications of the situation often. But they were unable to come up with any immediate solution.

Eddie had men and machinery to keep employed. And a growing fleet of lorries to keep on the road. What could he do?

Nothing at all for the moment, he discovered. Except pray.

Not only did the holiday-making couple discuss the situation back at home at some length, but they prayed about it with some sincerity.

They knew that the God in whom they had trusted as teenagers, and Who had showered them with numberless blessings throughout their lifetime, wouldn't let them down now.

He had, no doubt, some other, bigger, better plan for them.

But what? And how? And most importantly of all, when?

They had a month...

On Wednesday, Eddie and Nora drove south from Largs, home to Newlands Hill. To a rather dejected Anne.

They were still convinced though, that something, somehow was going to happen. It had before. And it would again, they were certain.

Just after lunch-time on Thursday, the phone rang. It was some-one from The Metal Box factory in Carlisle. Asking to speak to 'Mr. Eddie Stobart'.

When Eddie came to the phone the caller enquired, "Mr. Stobart, would you have a lorry available to come into our factory and take out a load of cans to be put into storage until they are required by the drinks manufacturers? If you could help us out until Christmas it would be a great help."

Eddie was interested. This could keep at least one lorry on the road. At least until Christmas. He was also somewhat curious.

"Why are you asking me?" he enquired. "Who told you about me?"

"Nobody really told me to call you specifically, Mr Stobart," the man's voice at the other end of the line went on to explain. "We are expecting to be very busy from now until Christmas and the transport manager has asked me to ring around all of the local haulage firms and see if they could help us out. Your name is one of six or seven I have underlined here in the telephone directory."

"Well, I'm sure we could manage to do something for you," Eddie replied, trying hard to disguise both his relief and his enthusiasm. "How many lorries would you need?"

Not knowing either how many lorries would be required, or for how long, the initial caller replied, "If you hold on there a minute I will put you through to our transport manager. He was the one who asked me to make these phone calls."

When the transport manager came on the line, he informed Eddie of the ongoing nature of the firm's transport requirements. The need to have thousands of empty cans transported out of the Metal Box factory in Carlisle. Some of these cans would require to be delivered to their major customers. The drinks manufacturers. And the remainder placed in storage. In order to leave room in the factory for thousands more cans. Which in turn would also have to be transported out to customers. Or placed in storage...

He then proceeded to explain how that with an 'increased volume of business at this time of year' their existing transport arrangements were proving inadequate.

When he had spent some time explaining the situation as best he could the manager then went on to repeat the question which he had instructed his junior to ask in the exploratory phone calls.

"Would you have a lorry there, Mr. Stobart? And would you be able to help us out with this problem we have? Until around Christmas time anyway?"

"Yes. I have a lorry available," Eddie was happy to report. "There will be one in with you tomorrow morning at nine o'clock."

When Eddie went out to the yard, after that phone call, he saw Edward and told him the good news. Edward was as keen for the business as his dad had been, and he had a number of questions to ask as to the practicalities of the situation. Were there, for instance, any special requirements with this new commodity they were being invited to transport?

There could be problems transporting drink cans in lorries normally used to ferry fertilizer, either in bags or in bulk. So Edward phoned back to Metal Box Ltd..

When he had spoken to the transport manager about the cans on the pallets, he and some of the other drivers in the yard set about a major conversion job on one of their trailers. They made temporary corner boards and cut special sheets to protect the load.

Only the best will do! This work, they all knew, if they could do it, keep it, and possibly increase it, would keep their drivers employed, at least until Christmas.

True to Eddie's promise, a six-wheeler Ford, the first Eddie Stobart Ltd. lorry to arrive at the gates of the Metal Box factory on business, was there at nine o'clock precisely, next morning. It collected, and then delivered, the first load for this new, but 'temporary', customer.

Soon the transport manager was on the phone asking for the use of another lorry. Then another.

By the end of November, when all of the basic-slag-for-Fisons operations out of Newlands Hill had ceased, the lorries of Eddie Stobart Ltd. were drawing loads out of the Carlisle factory daily.

Eddie's God had seen him through. Again. And had been, as usual, three or four moves ahead. Had prepared to meet the need, before it had even become known.

Initially, the company had gone into the Metal Box factory in Carlisle, to help out with a transportation problem. Until 'around Christmas time', 1973.

And although the work ceased again in January, 1974, a valuable initial contact had been made.

One that could prove useful in the future.

27

FORGING FORWARD

❖

During the mid-1970's the operations of Eddie Stobart Ltd. advanced significantly on three different fronts. Like a main road that splits up into three. The original road continues straight ahead. Perhaps not just as 'main' as it used to be. From the junction two others go ahead, also.

Each from a different side.

Each in a different direction.

Each to a different destination.

The 'main road', the original business, the fertilizer spreading, still continued. But with a difference. Fisons had ceased to use the Stobart monster store and one of the principal reasons for this was probably that basic slag had gradually been replaced in the market-place and on the pastures of Britain by granular fertilizer. This new product still had to be shipped, stored, sold, and spread, however. To keep this aspect of the company as profitable as it had always been, Eddie Stobart, agricultural merchant, negotiated the purchase of lorry-loads of this bagged fertiliser from the boat-loads which were being imported through Heysham docks.

This he transported to Newlands Hill and there he stored and from there he spread, as he had always done.

So Nora still had her little on-top-of-everything-else duty to perform as well. Moving men around to match up with the movement of machinery from farm to farm.

The first major off-shoot of that original enterprise was the use of some of the lorries to develop a haulage side to the business. No-one knew it then, but it was this particular 'side-road', emanating from the original 'junction', that was to develop, figuratively, into a dual-carriageway. And then a four-lane motorway.

A number of local manufacturers were so satisfied with the reliable service they were being afforded from this new company whom they had employed to transport their products that they continued to increase the number of loads carried out of their factories by them every month. This, in turn, lead to the purchase of more vehicles by Eddie Stobart Ltd., to cope with the growing demand. Which, in its turn, entailed the employing of more drivers for the new vehicles.

It soon became clear to the family that this transport operation had outgrown its base at Newlands Hill. The yard had long since proved inadequate to accommodate the increasing numbers of vehicles overnighting there. Late at night the way to the back door had become a have-to-walk-sideways path between closely-parked red-and- green lorries!

Something would have to be done.

On looking around for a new and suitable site from which to operate, Eddie discovered that a workshed and yard in Greystone Road, Carlisle, was to let. So he hired it. This particular site was ideally suited to his needs at that time, in two ways. Both in size, and situation. In size because it afforded ample parking for at least twenty-five trucks. And in situation for it was much closer to Carlisle's industrial sites than Newlands Hill had been.

This new depot required a full time manager who could be there every day to administer the ever-increasing volume of business. This responsibility was willingly undertaken by Edward, who had already begun to supervise the haulage operations from Newlands Hill, and who had, by that time also, been allocated his shares in the company. He was both keen and capable. An obvious 'man for the job'.

The third arm of the business, the other road away from 'Newlands Hill junction', was the increase both in popularity and profitability of the Farm, Home and Garden shop in Wigton. The townspeople had been impressed with the new venture with its fresh front, tidy interior, and extensive range of supplies for house or land. So they supported it, when the need arose.

Again, Eddie was not free to spend all day, every day or any day, in the shop. There was always something requiring his immediate and urgent attention. If it wasn't a meeting with a potential customer, it was a shipment of fertilizer to be hauled from Heysham. Or perhaps a spreader out of action outside Aspatria. It seemed that every new day that dawned brought with it some new need to be met. Or difficulty to be dealt with... So Ken Fearon, Anne's husband, became shop manager.

Gradually this shop had also to engage more staff as the extent and quality of its service became known. Soon there were three women and another man, in addition to Ken, working there, all the time.

With the seemingly unending expansion of the company, Eddie Stobart Ltd., in a variety of ways, its founder kept impressing upon his employees, both in word and by example, his unwritten code of practice. It was something he had learnt from older, wiser men, many years before. In a greenhouse. Then up a ladder.

Whether it was spreading fertilizer on fields, carrying cans out of Carlisle, or buying, then selling, fencing posts, pots and pans, or seed potatoes, it was always the same...

Only the best will do.

28

WHAT IS MAN ...?

❖

It was the Spring Bank Holiday weekend, 1973. Dr. Martyn Lloyd-Jones and his wife, Bethan, arrived at Newlands Hill on the Friday night for the weekend of well-advertised, much-anticipated and widely-supported meetings.

The couple from London hadn't long arrived in their rural retreat when William, who was just eleven years old but numbered 'The Doctor' as they had come to know him, affectionately, and his wife, amongst his closest buddies, asked them, "Would you like to come in and see our nice new sitting-room suite?"

Ever gracious, and always interested in all that was going on, anywhere, Dr. Lloyd-Jones replied instantly, "Oh yes, William, we would just love to see your new sitting room suite."

With that William led a procession into the sitting-room where everybody looked at, then sat on to try, the new leather suite.

Anxious to hear their reaction, but impatient in the absence of any immediate response, William asked, "Well, do you like it?"

"Yes, indeed. It is lovely. And very comfortable too," Mrs. Lloyd Jones assured him, kindly.

That was great. William thought so as well. But he hadn't finished with his honoured guests yet. There was just one further piece of information that he wanted to furnish them with. Something he felt they ought to know. To complete the picture of the sitting room suite.

"Yes, it's nice, isn't it?" he went on, happily. "And Ian and Margaret, our neighbours, gave mum and dad a hundred pounds for the old one!"

Nora was affronted.

She blushed to the roots of her hair. When William noticed her embarrassment he couldn't understand what she was so worried about. He was just sharing with his friends!

'The Doctor' was very sedate. And also very sensitive. Sensing a mother's mortification he remarked casually, and with a conciliatory smile, "So it worked out well for everybody then."

And the matter was declared closed.

His intuitive sensitivity in dealing with a potentially embarrassing situation was only one of a number of ways in which the stature of Dr. Martyn Lloyd-Jones, not only as an eminent Christian teacher, but also as a warm and caring gentleman was to be demonstrated over that particular weekend.

From their very first visit to Newlands Hill, three years previously, Dr. Lloyd-Jones and his wife had become close friends of the family. And on that 1973 visit 'The Doctor' helped cement that relationship. Especially with the boys.

John, Edward and William had their own special room in which they could relax and watch TV. They had been well warned however, that if they must put the TV on over the weekend it would have to be kept turned down very low. In order not to disturb 'the preacher', and his wife. They would 'have no time for that kind of thing.'

The boys had to have the TV on, though. Preacher or no preacher. For there was a snooker tournament on over the Bank Holiday weekend. And they loved to watch the snooker.

It was to their great surprise, then, on the Saturday night, after the meeting in the cleaned-up brushed-out fertilizer store, for the biggest tent they could possibly hire had long since proved too small for the crowds that had begun to come to the meetings, that the door of their 'den' was pushed open, gently.

"Do you mind if I join you for a while, boys?" came the request. It was Dr. Lloyd-Jones. "What are you watching?"

"Oh it's just the snooker," Edward explained, almost apologetically, and rose to make towards the set. And the off-button.

"Please don't switch it off," their unexpected guest begged. "I just love to watch the snooker."

He then settled himself into an armchair and sat for the remainder of that programme. Watching snooker. And discussing it knowledgeably with his hosts.

That meant a lot to those lads. Here was someone who could not only speak in such profound depths about the Bible but could also sit at ease with them in their 'den' and converse comfortably about blues and blacks and breaks. This man who was a recognised authority on the canon of scripture actually knew about cannons in snooker too!

It impressed them more than a week of preaching or a weekend of Bible teaching ever could. He was their friend. He was prepared to relate to them. At their level. So he commanded their respect.

Over the weekend people flocked to Newlands Hill. To hear Dr. Martyn Lloyd-Jones speak. And this drawing power was indicative of another aspect of the greatness of the man who had become a valued Stobart family friend and also someone whom every Christian in Cumberland seemed to want to hear. It was his ability to present an in-depth insight into the Scriptures in an acceptable and understandable, but always challenging, manner.

The Bank Holiday Monday address on 28th May, 1973, was particularly memorable to most of those who attended.

The resident sparrows, who sheltered from the north country wind and rain on the beams and ledges of the Stobart store, and could never understand why their home was invaded for three or four days in early summer by a crowd of preaching and singing happy humans, decided to chirp along in accompaniment as Dr. Martyn-Lloyd Jones announced his text for that meeting.

"I want to talk to you this evening about this beautiful little Psalm. Psalm 8. And I want to concentrate especially on verses three and four. 'When I consider thy heavens, the work of thy fingers, the moon and the stars, which thou hast ordained; What is man, that thou art mindful of him? and the son of man that thou visitest him?'

His cultivated voice had already hushed the capacity congregation into rapt attention.

In the course of his address Dr. Martyn Lloyd-Jones identified the three main lessons which he wanted his audience to learn from his chosen text.

The first was the greatness and majesty of God. And the universe.

"Scientists would try to tell us that this world of ours occurred by chance. After a mysterious 'big bang' sometime, somewhere, in the distant ages of the past. What nonsense! We Christians find it much simpler to believe what the Bible says in Genesis chapter one. 'In the beginning **God** created the heaven and the earth'..." The depth of emphasis on the word 'God' as he trilled it out left no one in any doubt as to the speaker's mind on the matter.

The second significant thought which Dr. Martyn Lloyd-Jones pointed out from Psalm 8, vs. 3,4, was what he called 'the unique position of man'. After describing with a witty scorn, the theory of evolution, he enquired, "Tell me, is it not a lot easier to believe the Bible's account of man's place in the universe? Listen to it while I read it to you. It is in our Psalm. Verses four and five. 'For thou hast made him a little lower than the angels, and hast crowned him with glory and honour. Thou madest him to have dominion over the works of thy hands; thou hast put all things under his feet:'..."

Having accorded both God and man what he considered to be their correct and scriptural places in the universe, Dr. Lloyd-Jones proceeded to present his spell-bound audience with the main thrust of his message.

"What then is the problem with man?" he enquired. "Man is such a puzzle. He is a massive contradiction! Let me explain to you what I mean. On July, 20th., 1969, men landed on the surface of the moon. In a capsule. Which had been propelled by a rocket, launched from Earth. And everybody exclaimed 'Isn't man wonderful? There is nothing that man cannot do!' Yet there is something which man cannot do. He cannot control his desires and passions. His basic instinct...

On July 21st, 1969, I came down to breakfast. I just happened to be in America at the time. And the newspaper heading was in bold type, Man has landed on the Moon. Wonderful! But on that very same page, in a heading in identically bold type was the account of the death of a poor girl in the car of senator Edward Kennedy in a lake up in Massachusetts. A terrible moral scandal.

Yes, man can do marvellous things. Yet man cannot control his rebellious nature. For man's nature is sinful. Man has sinned against God..."

Having spent a few moments outlining the problem in some detail, 'The Doctor' then turned to the solution.

"What is the answer to the problem of man and his sin? Can man be changed? And if so, **how** can he be changed?" he enquired.

"The answer is in our Psalm, too. Listen. 'What is man that thou art **mindful** of him. And the son of man that thou **visitest** him?' There it is. There is the solution. God is still 'mindful' of us. He thinks about us. And what's more he has visited us...

Do you know what is the only hope for the world tonight? It lies in a series of LAUNCHINGS. You know what I mean by a 'launching', don't you? We were given a date for the launching of the rocket to the moon. And on that precise date the men climbed into their capsule. Then the rocket was launched and we watched it go up and up and up," the old man's voice rose to a crescendo, and his finger rose upward too as he spoke, "to the moon. Then we saw the men climb out of their capsule on the surface of the moon. Their mission had been successful...

Well, let us put our old Gospel in a more modern context. Listen to this, 'When the fulness of the time was come, God sent forth his Son, made of a woman, made under the law..' Now let me give you another translation. 'When the fulness of the time was come God **launched** his Son..' It's the same idea. 'Sent forth, launched'. God launched His Son into this world. And what's more He launched Him in a capsule. He was 'made of a woman'. The capsule was a virgin's womb. From that capsule our blessed Lord Jesus Christ stepped out onto the surface of this planet.

Then, did you ever wonder what he came for? Was it to collect a few samples of rock and conduct a few experiments? No! That's not why He came! He told us Himself why He came. He said, 'The Son of man is come to seek and to save that which was lost'. He came to rescue us. To save us from our sin. And He walked up and down on this earth, enduring the contradiction of sinners against Himself. Then eventually they caught Him and crucified Him on the cross of Calvary. After His death they took Him down from the cross and placed Him in Joseph's new tomb.

They encapsulated him again! But was that the end? No! God sent the rocket of resurrection to burst open that tomb and He came out, and ascended again to the throne of His Father on high...

Tell me this, did the events of 20th July, 1969, ever make you think of this launching? This visitation of God to earth? Well, if didn't it should have. And I'll tell you why...

You have another launching coming up. It will be when God places his Rocket of Death beneath this capsule which you call your body. And launches you out into a great and vast eternity. Tell me, are you prepared for that? We all watched with great interest and anticipation as the astronauts made meticulous preparations for their journey to the moon. We would have considered them stupid if they hadn't undergone rigorous training, and made careful preparations.. Yet so many people make no preparations whatsoever for their final journey. Their last launching...

Let me tell you of two differences between you and those American astronauts.

The first is that they knew the exact day of their launch. Indeed we were told some six months beforehand the exact date, and the exact second when those men would step out onto the surface of the moon! But you and I don't know the day of our death. We don't know when our soul is going to be launched from our bodies. Tell me my friend, have you made any preparation at all for **that?**

Then there's a second difference. You will remember that before that successful launch in 1969 there were a number of attempted launches that didn't work. They never got off the ground. So what happened? The scientists said, 'Oh we must have made a mistake. We will try again.' That's how science works. By experimenting and learning from one's mistakes. You see they had a second chance. They could correct their mistake. But my friend with the rocket of death there is no second chance. It will be too late then to start making preparations. The Bible says NOW is the time 'Behold now is the accepted time. Behold now is the day of salvation..'"

Dr. Martyn Lloyd-Jones, obviously drained by the effort of it all, then concluded his address with an impassioned plea for souls to come to the Saviour. While there was time. While God was still calling. For after death there would be no second chance.

As he stepped down from the platform an awesome stillness enveloped the building. The people sat mesmerised. They were lost in thought. Many were struggling with the truth of what they had just heard. God was at work .

Even the sparrows had fallen silent.

Everyone in that building that May evening had been treated to a wonderful exposition, and a marvellous insight into the subject, 'What is man?'

They had also been presented with an unavoidable challenge.

29

THE HABIT OF THE RABBIT

❖

During the latter years of the 1970's the business of Eddie Stobart Ltd. progressed and expanded satisfactorily in all its aspects. The transport under Edward's management, the shop under Ken's management, and the fertilizer haulage and spreading under the watchful eye of Eddie himself.

In 1979, however, Eddie Stobart was approached by a Carlisle contractor who informed him that he had a large site available on the Kingstown industrial estate in the city. Not only had he the site available but his firm, Border Steel Ltd., also had the equipment and expertise to erect a substantial building on the site should Eddie require it.

Eddie promised to give his proposal serious consideration without letting him know that he had been contemplating the feasibility of just such a project for some time. He knew that the store to which his company was at that time transporting cans for the Metal Box company was unsuitable for its purpose in a number of ways. The main two reasons were that it was too far from the factory and it was not entirely hygienic. It was a disused R.A.F. hangar, ten miles west of the city. And it had a leaking roof! So the storeman had to be careful where he placed the pallets of empty cans or he could find them filled prematurely! Eddie realized that with the tightening of legislation in relation to the hygienic production of both food and drink, it wouldn't be long until that particular store would be classed as unfit for use.

He had given some thought, too, to the possible site of a new store should he ever consider either leasing or building a new one. He had examined all aspects of that matter carefully, also. This ability to assess all the points pertaining to any situation was something Eddie had learnt as a boy in the fields around Hesket Newmarket. Trapping rabbits. A wise old farmer had once told him that before he ever caught a single rabbit he ought to study the animals. Find out where they had their burrows. What time of the day, or night, they were most likely to be out and about. Where and when they fed. Everything about them. Know them through and through. Become familiar with, as the old man had described it, 'the habit of the rabbit'.

So it was with the Metal Box Co., for example. They had a pattern of movement and a variety of specific requirements. Eddie knew that they were manufacturing in both Glasgow and Carlisle. And his company were being asked to transport cans to an increasing number of factories all over Britain, using the ever-expanding network of motorways.

So a new store in Kingstown, on the north side of the city of Carlisle, and within a mile of the M6, would be an ideal site on which to erect a big modern store. Couldn't be better.

Having convinced himself that a new building in which local manufacturers could store their waiting-to-be-delivered products would be a viable business project, Eddie returned to the contractor who had made the initial approach to him, and asked him for an estimate of cost.

On receiving the contractor's estimate for the erection of a store of large-enough-to-be-worthwhile proportions, Eddie made another discovery. It came as quite a shock to him to realize that to set his plan in motion was going to require significant and effective action in the field of finances. Effective action which could affect their whole style of living. He would have to sell both the premises at Newlands Hill and the shop in Wigton.

Convinced as he was that this was the correct course of action, to develop the business, Eddie and Nora sold their bungalow and all the outbuildings of the sprawling Newlands Hill complex to Eddie's brother Ronnie, who in turn let the bungalow to their son John and his new wife, Christine. Eddie also sold the shop in Wigton to a local butcher, and Ken and Anne, on being relieved of the responsibility for the shop set up their own business, K. & A. Fearon, continuing in a family tradition. Buying, selling, and spreading fertilizer.

Eddie and Nora then moved house, settling in Suttle Close in the city of Carlisle, not far from the Kingstown industrial estate.

Now Eddie had the two basic essentials to advance his proposed new project. He had both the vision and the financial capacity to carry it through. And his move in from the country meant that he also had the added bonus of being close at hand. To oversee operations when building began.

Plans were drawn up for a store extending to 64000 sq. feet of floor area. Careful consideration had also been given to the height of the store to maximize its storage capacity. Metal Box packed their cans on pallets, which, when loaded, stood nine feet high. This new store was designed to be twenty-seven feet high at the eaves, so that it could accommodate three pallets stacked on top of one another.

The habit of the rabbit, again!

When these plans had been submitted to the Carlisle City Council, and approved, the way was clear for building to commence. So on Friday, 14th March, 1980, the heavy machinery moved onto the site.

The work had begun on what was to be Eddie Stobart's largest single business enterprise, to date.

In May, Dr. Martyn Lloyd-Jones, and his wife Bethan came to stay for a few days with their friends, Eddie and Nora. 'The Doctor' was eighty years of age by then, and frail, but he had promised to speak at a conference in Glasgow on Friday, 9th May. Since he hadn't spoken publicly for some time he asked Eddie if he could arrange a meeting for him somewhere around Carlisle. So that he could try himself out on a sympathetic audience. Eddie was happy to comply with the old man's request and he and Nora were also delighted to have the couple to stay with them once more.

On the Saturday morning, 3rd May, Eddie and Nora took Dr Lloyd-Jones and Bethan out for a run in the car, and 'The Doctor', still as-ever interested in all that was going on, suggested that they go and have a look at the Kingstown site.

Again happy to comply with such a gentleman's request, Eddie took them there. On arriving at the Saturday-silent site they found that the most of the steelwork had been erected and the concrete footings for the brickwork had been 'poured'.

As he drove in Eddie wondered what interest a medical doctor who was also an eminent theologian and Bible teacher would have in steel girders and concrete footings, but he had expressed himself anxious to see the work so far. So see it he would. Wrapped in his overcoat, even though it was a reasonably pleasant day, Dr. Lloyd-Jones walked slowly around part of that site, observing everything with his eagle eye. Then he turned to his host, and said unusually abruptly, "Very good, Eddie. Very good. I think we will get back in the car now."

Interested though he was in everything 'The Doctor' was not now physically capable of any exertion. The spirit was willing, but the flesh was weak. And weakening, rapidly.

Through the summer of 1980, and then on into the autumn, the men and machines of Border Steel Ltd., and a number of other sub-contractors, worked away at Kingstown.

In the dark days of approaching winter the building was nearing completion. It just required the 'finishing touches.'

One of these finishing touches was the final 'skim' on the massive concrete floors. A succession of groaning, tumbling, churning cement-mixers had poured their sloshy contents on to the floor during the day. Then when this concrete was at a particular stage of setting it needed to be finally finished off. 'Skimmed'.

With the pressure on to have yet more of the floor 'poured' every day the best time for skimming the already-ready sections of the floor seemed to be in the middle of the night.

This job was undertaken, voluntarily, by William, who was then nineteen years of age and extremely interested in both fast cars and the family business. Like his father before him too, he wasn't one to shirk a bit of hard or prolonged manual work.

So, much to her dismay, mother Nora used to hear her son William rise at four o'clock on a black December morning, much as his father had done almost twenty years before, and slip out into the darkness. When she heard his car drive away off, up the road to Kingstown, she used to lie awake, worried sick, until she heard his key in the lock again...

All sorts of thoughts besieged her mind.

'Will he not be lonely up in that big empty building, all on his own? Why does he not ask somebody to help him? Even if they didn't do much they would at least be company. What if somebody attacks him?...'

The heart of a mother!

As for William, he was quite happy! He loved the skilled work of skimming. The unrestricted space of the empty-echoing store. And he could just imagine the end result. A busy store reverberating with a succession of shouted instructions and the hum of fork-lift trucks.

And he returned home, too, despite his mother's night-time nightmare nervousness. Often exhausted, but always safely!

All the planning and hard work was soon to pay dividends, for on 10th December, 1980, the first load of cans, from Metal Box, Glasgow, arrived for storage in the new Eddie Stobart depot, in Kingstown industrial estate, Carlisle. Early in 1981 both the Carlisle and Glasgow factories of Metal Box were using the lorries of Eddie Stobart Ltd. for some of their transport and the new building at Kingstown for their storage. And that was only the beginning.

In the next few years the haulage side of the business developed rapidly and the 64000 sq.foot warehouse was found to be too small to meet the ever growing demand for storage space. So Eddie went back to Carlisle County Council and leased an adjoining piece of land from them. On this he built another store, thus increasing the storage capacity of the company to 80000 sq. feet.

When the new building was complete, Eddie Stobart and son Edward did a tour of inspection. As they walked back towards the office block, Edward looked back at the new building, then turned to his father and said, gratefully, "Thank you, dad. I can manage now!"

He could, too.

And has done!

30

THERE'S A GOOD PREACHER HERE TONIGHT!

❖

When Dr. Martyn Lloyd Jones phoned in mid-April, 1980, to say that he had been invited to speak in Glasgow in early May, and had accepted the invitation, he also requested two things. He asked that Bethan and he be permitted to break their journey northward with their old friends in Carlisle, and that Eddie should arrange a meeting for him in the Church in Wigton, if possible. 'The Doctor' said that he would like to become accustomed to the sound of his own voice again, having been silent for some time because of ill-health.

When they heard these simple requests Eddie and Nora were overjoyed at the prospect of having their old friends to stop over with them in their new home in Carlisle. They would also love to hear 'The Doctor' speak again, if he was at all able, but they were well aware that the Union Street Evangelical Church in Wigton would be far too small to accommodate all the others from all around who would also love to hear him speak as well. It only seated about one hundred people and there was very little room for parking. Totally inadequate for such an occasion.

On making enquiries about a larger , more suitable venue, Eddie obtained the use of the Methodist Central Hall in Carlisle, for an 8.15 p.m. meeting on the evening of Sunday, 4th May.

Since this meeting was hurriedly arranged there was little time for an extensive advertising campaign, but it didn't really seem to matter. One single advertisement in the local paper and the magic of word of mouth worked wonders!

Long before the arranged starting time of the meeting people were queueing in the street to get into the Methodist Central Hall. They had to wait for the usual evening service to finish, and then there occurred the brief and annoying-for-those-who-were-in-it but amusing-for-those-who-were-watching-it situation where a relatively small congregation trying to leave the building was met by a much larger crowd trying to enter it. However, the frustration for all was only fleeting, and the Methodist Central Hall was soon to play host to the largest congregation it had seen for many years.

As Nora and Bethan approached the door of the building, a chap called Harry whose daytime job was to operate the lifts in the Binns store in Carlisle, came rushing up behind the two ladies. He was red-faced and out of breath. A sidelong glance had obviously revealed to him that he knew one of them. Nora. He had seen her at his work.

When he had taken a few sidesteps he addressed them both, panting, "I say, ladies, they tell me there is a good preacher on here tonight! Do you know who it is?"

Nora had just her mouth open to answer him when Harry-in-a-hurry dashed on. To make sure he found a seat up near the front somewhere. To hear this 'good preacher'. Whoever he was!

Bethan could hardly speak for laughing. "Yes, I know who it is! I know him!" she repeated in amusement, long after Harry had been swallowed up in the crowds surging towards the door.

By the time 8.15 p.m. came the Hall was packed with almost seven hundred people, all waiting in eager anticipation to hear Dr. Martyn Lloyd-Jones.

The pulpit in the Methodist Central Hall in Carlisle was very high. When standing in it, the speaker almost faced the gallery. It also meant, however, that the preacher had to climb a number of steps to get up there. Fine for a fellow in his forties, but a different proposition for an ailing man of eighty.

The capacity crowd watched with sympathetic respect as Eddie Stobart helped that elderly Bible-teacher up those steps. The effort was to prove a severe drain on the limited physical resources of an old man.

When the arduous ascent in the hushed Hall was complete 'The Doctor' lowered himself gently into a pulpit chair. Mopping the perspiration from the exertion from his brow he looked around from his vantage point. Surveyed the expectant crowd who had gravitated towards that gathering from all arts and parts. Just to hear him speak.

After Eddie had led the meeting and welcomed the large congregation, he introduced and welcomed Dr. Martyn Lloyd-Jones. Then to a reverential silence, Eddie helped the physically weak but mentally alert and spiritually strong old gentleman across to the lectern.

Placing his Bible before him he announced his text for the evening. "I want to read to you just one verse from the Book of Acts. It is in chapter eleven and it is verse sixteen..." he began. Then, after reading aloud the complete verse, 'The Doctor' went on, "My text for this evening is there in the last part of that verse. 'The disciples were called Christians first in Antioch'".

Gripping the pulpit rails on either side of the reading desk tightly with frail and shaking hands, Dr. Martyn Lloyd-Jones raised his eyes and silently but studiously scanned the vast audience. Then he continued, "What we have read together is the first mention of Christians in the Bible."

There followed a brief pause to allow that fact to sink in, before he resumed with what was on his heart, "So now, you good people, what I want to do this evening is to tell you exactly what it means to be a Christian ..."

And then he proceeded to do just that.

Clearly. Sincerely.

Simply. Earnestly.

For the next forty-five minutes.

In the course of that memorable address the respected aged Bible teacher perspired freely, and his voice trembled occasionally, but he never lost his train of thought or his clarity of presentation.

The audience were transfixed. Spellbound. Hanging on his every word. It seemed that both the preacher and the people were surrounded by a strange sense of the presence of God.

It was awesome.

When Dr. Martyn Lloyd-Jones sat down at the close of his address, nobody moved, or coughed, or shuffled. There was none of the usual now-that-that's-over-when-do we-get-out? kind of relieved unrest.

Everybody sat motionless. Just hoping that somehow, or for some reason, the exhausted old man of God would return to the lectern, grab hold of the rails, and start all over again...

But it didn't happen. And they had to go home, reluctantly.

As that vast crowd waited in the aisles for their turn to spill out onto the streets of Carlisle, every single person was left in no doubt whatsoever about two things. The first was, what it meant to be a Christian. Many hearts were touched that night. Dr. Martyn Lloyd Jones hadn't made an appeal. He hadn't very often ever done throughout his preaching career, claiming that his whole message was an appeal. At the close of that evening some people had become Christians for the very first time. And some people who had been Christians for years had the challenge to live for the God whom they claimed to serve, dramatically renewed.

The second sobering thought which every member of that in-a-peculiar-way-privileged congregation came away with that May evening was the conviction that they had heard 'The Doctor' speak in Carlisle for the very last time.

They were to be proved right, too.

Dr. Martyn Lloyd-Jones addressed very few public meetings after that.

For the next few months his health deteriorated steadily and by the end of that year he was a very ill man, confined to the house.

In mid-February, 1981, when Eddie rang up to enquire about him, it was Mrs. Lloyd-Jones, Bethan, who answered the phone.

Eddie said, "Hello, Bethan, I know you must be busy there but Nora and I were wondering about the Doctor. How is he today?"

"He is very weak, Eddie," was the concerned reply. "Has been for..."

She stopped abruptly in mid-sentence.

When she came back on the line she said, "Just a minute, Eddie. He is indicating that he wants to speak to you."

With that Mrs. Lloyd-Jones took the telephone across to her very frail husband and held the receiver for him while he spoke. The Doctor's first words, almost inaudible, spoken in a faint and husky voice were, "Eddie, how are you?"

"I'm all right, Doctor. But it is you we are concerned about. More importantly, how are you?" Eddie replied.

"I am near the glory, Eddie. Don't you worry about me. You are still in the battle. I am praying for you..." The old man's feeble voice tailed off into silence. It was all he could manage.

It was almost too much for him.

That assurance that 'The Doctor' was praying for him were the last words that Eddie heard from his close friend and Christian counsellor. For in the early hours of the morning on 1st March, 1981, Dr. Martyn Lloyd-Jones passed peacefully into the presence of the One he had served so diligently throughout his lifetime. To the acclaim of the Master, "Well done, good and faithful servant."

Perhaps it wouldn't be straining the bounds of possibility to their absolute limit, either, to suppose that a ripple of whisper, like a soft wind through standing wheat, swept amongst the angelic beings in that Haven of Rest, "There's a good preacher here tonight!"

31

GO FOR IT BIG

❖

Eddie was full of the story. He had joined his son Edward for lunch, one day in 1981, out from their Portacabin offices in Kingstown, Carlisle, and was sharing one of his that-morning experiences.

"I had a financial rep. in with me there before lunch, Edward," he reported enthusiastically. "He is moving away from the district and came to see me before leaving. He told me that there was something different about me from most of the other people he has come across in business. I had been a pleasure to deal with. I drove a hard bargain, he said, but he didn't mind that. There was no bad language, and he said that he had found me to be absolutely straight in all of my dealings. That gave me the chance to witness to him, tell him I was a Christian, and give him a Gideon Testament..."

Edward knew his dad. He respected his fervour for God and in Christian things, but he also had the burden of a business on his mind.

"Hold on a minute there, Dad. Calm down," he cautioned. "Did you ever think that you couldn't have done that if I hadn't been running around looking after the business?"

It was true. And it was also an indication of the direction in which each of their separate lives was to move in the next ten years.

Eddie, father, continued to look after his warehousing interests, but increasingly on a part-time basis, as he had begun to devote more and more of his time to his compelling major interest. Christian work. The activities of the Y.M.C.A. in Carlisle, the Gideon movement, Billy Graham rallies...

Edward, son, became progressively more concerned for the future of the transport business. At that time he was experiencing great difficulty in securing sufficient haulage contracts to keep his drivers busy. The country was in the grip of a recession. There were months when some of the drivers worked one-week-on-and-one-week-off with half of the lorries parked up. Two or three of the men were kept busy with odd jobs around the yard. Cleaning up lorries that weren't going anywhere.

Although they were doing some work for Metal Box in Carlisle, amongst others, it wasn't enough to keep everyone busy. In those days a number of larger haulage contractors worked for the can-making company, and they had a small fleet of their own vehicles, so Eddie Stobart Ltd. were only called upon at busy times. Like over the summer period, or in the month before Christmas. Or they were also offered all the work that nobody else wanted. At nights or over the weekend.

Edward worked hard. In management during the day trying to organize the loads, and secure more work. Then he did most of the weekend and night-time driving himself.

When Edward's younger brother, William, turned twenty-one years of age, he started to drive a truck. And he loved it, too. The power of the truck and the challenge of the distance. Mile after mile out on the open road. What freedom! He reckoned that it was great to get paid for doing something he loved so much!

Then, in 1984, Edward bought premises in Kingstown, beside his father's storage facility, and moved all twenty-eight trucks and the repair and maintenance garage over there. This could only help to improve efficiency with the entire operation based on a single site.

William had been driving, and thoroughly enjoying the experience for three years, when Edward realized that something needed to be done. There were problems to be addressed. The business was keeping all the staff busy, but that was about all it was doing. It wasn't really making an acceptable profit.

Edward became frustrated, and voiced his concerns to William one day. It was a crisis talk. Make our minds up time.

"We have a choice, William," he outlined the situation to his younger brother, bluntly. "Either we fold Eddie Stobart Ltd., and each of us takes a wagon and goes it on his own, or else we make a real push, go for it big, and try to get more work. Build up this business together. Which will it be?"

After some discussion they decided upon the latter option. To 'go for it big'.

So the first move they made, in August 1986, was to employ more staff. Experts to look at means of developing the company, and procuring more business. And someone to take care of personnel management.

Later in that year, also, Edward persuaded William to join him in the office. For good. William had tried working in the office a year or so previously but had only lasted six months. He had pleaded to be allowed behind the wheel again and Edward had relented. The regular routine and constant confinement of office life had just been too difficult to cope with, he found, after the relative pleasure and freedom, for him, of driving all over Britain.

Now this was different. For two reasons. Firstly, the nature of the work he was being asked to do. Having been asked to assume responsibility for the traffic desk, he found the work rewarding. Challenging, even. After all, the next best thing to driving a truck yourself must be to use your accumulated experience of the country to decide on routes, and calculate costs and mileage.

The second reason that he settled more readily in the office, second time around, was one of the heart. William had met a girl whom he liked, and he wanted to spend more time with her. So trips to places like London, Bristol or Southampton weren't as appealing to him as they once had been. Indeed he was planning to get married within a year or two, so the extra salary in his new position would prove very useful, as well.

After his brother had joined him in management, Edward began to market the company seriously. Daily. And diligently. He was aware of the fact that with their decision to employ extra staff and to focus on expansion, Eddie Stobart Ltd. was now in a 'make-or-break' 'sink-or-swim' situation.

It was during those days that an opportunity with an obvious growth potential came to his attention. He heard that the management of Metal Box Ltd. had decided to sell their own few vehicles and employ one single haulier to handle all of their transport requirements. Edward was convinced that with their fleet of vehicles, and storage capacity, Eddie Stobart Ltd. could meet any of that company's conditions.

When he enquired as to why his firm hadn't been invited to tender for the contract, he was informed that they were considered 'too small'. This only served to stiffen Edward's resolve. He continued to request a tender form until he was eventually furnished with one. Probably to 'keep him quiet'!

After some days of careful consideration and detailed calculations Edward and his management team submitted their tender. And had it accepted. Eddie Stobart Ltd. were awarded the contract.

It wasn't the only one, however. Edward continued to press for more business. In those days, long before mobile phones, fax machines or E.mail had been developed to their present level of usage, he made personal contact with a number of manufacturing outlets all across the north of England and into southern Scotland. Selling the services of Eddie Stobart Ltd., 'haulage specialists'.

And it paid off. As the name of the company became better known, and its reputation for a high standard of service became more widespread, so the orders began to come in. A trickle at first. Then a steady stream.

Eddie Stobart Ltd., had turned the corner. They were expanding. At last.

Then, in November, 1989, Eddie sold his store in Kingstown, where he had been warehousing in the eighties, to the company. This proved beneficial to both buyer and seller alike.

To Edward, William, and the company because they could continue to expand their operations. Continue to 'go for it big'. And bigger if they wished.

To Eddie himself also, for, whilst remaining as non-executive chairman of the company, thus maintaining his link with the firm, he had two other activities upon which he could quite happily engage his mind and energies.

The first of these was settling, with Nora, into the bungalow in the country, where they had moved to from Carlisle, in 1986. Out from the city, back into their beloved Cumbrian countryside again.

The second was even more important to Eddie.

He was now at liberty to concentrate almost full-time on his growing list of Christian pursuits.

32

I'M REALLY SCARED!

---❖---

I t was late 1990, and the Gulf War had just begun. The unrest in the Middle East was causing concern in the minds of many people. Right across the world. And the people of Britain were no exception.

This sense of uncertainty and trepidation surfaced one afternoon when Nora was in a dress shop in Carlisle. She went in there often, and felt she knew the staff well. Had always found them friendly and helpful.

It was the week just after hostilities in the Gulf had commenced. Full of sound and fury. The news was on everybody's lips. People spoke of it in fearful, hushed tones. Afraid that it could escalate into a global confrontation.

"Isn't it terrible, this war in Iraq?" Jackie Mc Call, who owned the shop, said to Nora.

"Indeed it is," Nora agreed. She could be no more certain of what was going to happen, than anybody else.

"I'm really scared!" Jackie went on. "What if it comes here? It could end up in a World War. We could all end up being killed!"

"You appear to be very frightened," Nora replied, detecting a deep sense of insecurity in the normally relaxed and carefree shop-owner's whole disposition.

"You are right, I am!" she confessed, unashamedly.

"Do you have a Bible, Jackie?" Nora went on. "The Bible predicts 'perilous times in the last days', but it also tells how we can have complete peace and reassurance in spite of all sorts of outside circumstances."

"No, I'm afraid I don't have a Bible," Jackie admitted. "Haven't had one since I was a little girl."

Nora produced, from her handbag, the Gideon New Testament which she always carried for such occasions.

Holding the little book out in front of her, she asked her friend, "If I give you this New Testament, Jackie, will you promise me that you will read it? There is a help section in the front of it here," she explained, showing it to the shop owner who by that time had leant across the counter for a better look. "These tell you where in the book to read to find help in a whole variety of different situations."

Jackie thanked Nora sincerely, took the proffered Testament gratefully, and promised to read it regularly.

While she had been talking to Jackie, Nora was aware that the two other shop assistants, Nancy and Mildred, had been attentive eavesdroppers to their conversation.

Sensing their interest, she turned to them. "Sorry ladies, I have only the one New Testament with me, but I will bring you each one next week if you would like," she volunteered.

The two shop assistants were pleased. And said they would love to have a New Testament. Next week.

True to her promise, Nora brought the two assistants, Nancy and Mildred, a New Testament each on the following Friday. She was pleased to see the delight with which those two women received the books. And she was also delighted to discover that Jackie had been reading hers, and telling them about it. So they just couldn't wait to get their hands on a copy.

Nora then started to make regular visits to that shop. On some of her visits she would buy something to wear, but whether she purchased anything or not it didn't seem to matter. There was invariably something of vital importance to be discussed. Like the progress of the War. Or the uncertainty surrounding what some of them called 'the end of the world.' Or the help each one of them was obtaining from reading the New Testaments.

On one such Friday of deep discussion, another lady, a customer well known to the staff, was sitting on a chair in the shop. And she soon became caught up in the conversation.

When she heard the shop-girls speak so confidently about what they had 'read in the Bible' she began to make a few enquiries for herself. How did they know so much about the Bible? And where had they obtained their Bibles from, anyway?

The answer to both of those questions for all of them was simple. And the same. They knew whatever it was that they knew, from reading the Gideon New Testaments, which had been given to them by Nora.

Unwilling to miss even the ghost of an opportunity to present yet another Testament to yet another interested enquirer, Nora explained, "I gave the girls in the shop here a New Testament each a few weeks ago. Would you like one, too?"

"Yes, indeed I would!" the lady replied. "These girls seem to be very keen to read theirs. And they seem to be finding them very helpful."

She was dead right in her observations.

They were. And they did.

Nora gave her the handbag copy which she never left the house without.

During the latter part of 1990, Nora's weekly visits to the shop became a highlight for the enquiring staff. They had begun to save up their questions on the New Testament and its teachings for her to answer. Her visits became progressively longer.

This pleased Nora in one respect. Upset her in another.

She was delighted at the girls' genuine interest in the Bible. And was surprised at the nature and depth of some of their questions. That was encouraging.

What wasn't so encouraging, however, was a fact that Nora well knew, from her earlier business experience. It was that no dress shop could possibly make a profit if the staff were spending more of their time studying the Bible than they were selling blouses.

It wasn't fair to Jackie.

So just before Christmas Nora made a suggestion to the shop-owner, and her staff. "If I started a Bible study out in my house once a month, say, in the New Year, would any of you be interested in coming?" she wondered. "Then we could talk as much as we liked and for as long as we liked and not keep you back from your work in here."

Jackie, Nancy and Mildred appeared overjoyed at the prospect.

"We would love to come!" they replied, almost in chorus. "And what about bringing others?"

"Oh yes, you can bring whoever you like!" Nora was in her turn thrilled with their genuinely enthusiastic response.

So, in January, 1991, Nora Stobart commenced a monthly Bible study for ladies in her home. All the women from the shop came, and brought two friends, Arabelle and Joan. They enjoyed it they said, and soon became regular attenders. When news of this friendly and informal Bible study session became known, the numbers attending increased, again. Jackie brought along her neighbour, Norma, an active Christian, and she in turn invited Heather and Margaret.

As the women of the group became comfortable with each other, the discussions became more lively. And the questions more penetrating.

Nora spent a considerable amount of time in prayer and preparation before each of those monthly gatherings. She wanted to have all the Scriptural answers for these ladies, if possible. They all seemed to be so diligently in search of peace. Satisfaction. And truth...

Then came the big breakthrough.

The long-awaited answer to prayer.

The study groups had been running for six months when, on Wednesday, 5th June, 1991, at a Billy Graham satellite rally in Carlisle, which they had attended instead of their regular meeting in Nora's home, Jackie and Joan both came to know the Lord Jesus Christ as their Saviour.

It was almost a year since Jackie had first expressed her fears about coming world events.

As she left the rally that night, still clutching one of her most prized possessions, she said emphatically, "I would never have come to this point, I would never have come to know the Lord, if it hadn't been for this little New Testament."

She then set off for home.

Saved. Satisfied. And serene.

Jackie wasn't scared any more.

33

GOD'S NOT SLEEPING, YOU KNOW

❖

Early in 1991, as Nora was planning to commence her monthly home Bible study sessions with the ladies from the shop in Carlisle, and some others, she and Eddie had a visit from two of their friends, Bert and Dorothy Williams.

As they chatted together Nora shared with them the Testament-talks-in-the-shop leading to Bible-studies-in-the-house story. They were intrigued. Whilst Nora was talking, Dorothy, who was at that time President of the Auxiliaries, the women's section of the Gideons, was thinking. Here is someone with particular qualities, she mused. A lady with a background of valuable experience in a caring role.

It gave her an idea. Prompted by God, through prayer.

"Nora, there's a vacancy coming up in May for a chaplain to the Auxiliaries. Would you consider allowing your name to go forward for it?" she asked.

"No, indeed I wouldn't," was Nora's immediate reaction. "There must be other women in the country far better qualified to hold such a post than me."

Dorothy wasn't to be deterred.

"Don't say that, Nora," she chastened. "I believe God has prepared you in many ways for just such a position. You have such wide experience. In business, with a family, in Christian work. Pray about it. Think about it. And I will keep in touch."

Sure enough Dorothy did keep in touch.

Almost a month later, just when Nora had begun to think that she had forgotten all about it, she rang again.

"Just wondering, Nora, If you had given any more thought to allowing your name to go forward for chaplain?" she enquired, kindly. Dorothy was convinced in her 'heart of hearts' that her friend was the person for the position, but she didn't want to force anything. Sound 'too pushy'.

In truth, Nora had been giving the matter some careful consideration in her pensive moments. It had flitted in and out of her mind. At all stages of the day and night. Like the swallows in the sheds at Newlands Hill. Gliding gracefully in and out. Making some long stays. And some short.

The problem about it was though that every time she considered it she came to a different conclusion!

Sometimes it was simple. If God wants me to do this, I will. No problem.

At other times it was more complex. Like, what would somebody, with a background like mine, do as chaplain to a national organization?

It was therefore hard to know how to answer Dorothy's question. What to say to be right.

There was also a third idea which she had considered. The compromise. The deferred option. Another seeking-for-a-sure-sign situation. And it was the one which she chose to voice to her pleasantly persistent friend.

"I have thought about this a lot, Dorothy," she began, truthfully, "and I will tell you what I have decided. All the Auxiliaries know that this post is coming vacant in May. If somebody from another Branch, asks me, without either your knowledge or prompting, then I will allow my name to go forward. For then I will be sure it is of God."

Dorothy was happy enough with that. It sounded reasonable enough to her. And the kind of discretion which Nora had shown in that situation convinced her completely, if ever she need to be convinced completely, that Nora was the right woman for the job. So she went away and started to pray, ever so earnestly, that someone else would contact her!

Ten days later the Stobart phone rang again. It was Winifred ('Win') Sheriston from the South Lakeland Gideon Branch, asking for Nora.

After the usual How-are-all-the-family? and What-about-the-meetings-in-your-Branch? ask-the-question-to-forget-the-answer introductions, Win got round to the point. The reason for her call.

"Three of us here have been talking about the post of chaplain to the Auxiliaries, which is coming up in May," she said. "And we were wondering if you would allow your name to go forward? We feel that you would be an ideal person for the job."

Nora was amazed at the wonderful ways and workings of God. She told Win of Dorothy Williams' earlier approach, and their agreement.

Now she had her answer.

Unmistakable. Indisputable. Undeniable.

For sure.

When Dorothy phoned again she told her what had happened. And agreed to be nominated as a potential chaplain to The Auxiliaries.

When Convention time came around, in early May, Nora was unopposed for the position. And declared elected.

For the next twelve months the new chaplain worked away conscientiously in her post. Writing to members passing through times of difficulty. Phoning, chatting, counselling.

It was a happy, busy period, but God had given her the time for it, as the family were, by then, all married and away from home. She also had the experience of life, with all that she had been through since childhood.

Nora's greatest challenge of her three years in office loomed up ahead for her, though. It came before the Annual Convention a year later. In May, 1992.

Then Nora was expected to speak to the Auxiliaries. Bring them an appropriate spiritual message. A kind of an I-want-to-push-you-on-to-greater-things-while-patting-your-back-at-the-same-time talk. And there would be hundreds there!

This wasn't going to be like one of her home Bible studies. Nor was it going to be like having a cosy fireside chat with a crestfallen colleague. Or a one-to-one telephone ministry.

This was standing up on her feet addressing a capacity congregation who would be expecting something special! And she certainly wasn't Dr. Martyn-Lloyd Jones! Or even Eddie, who was also quite used to that kind of thing.

As the weekend of the convention approached, Nora became increasingly perplexed. She was so nervous about her public-speaking appointment that she considered resigning from her post as chaplain...

There was no way she could go through with this, she felt.

She didn't resign, however. And Eddie and she travelled south to Birmingham for the Convention.

On the Friday night before the Saturday of the chaplain's address, Nora lay in bed, wide awake. Tossing and turning. What was she going to do? Although she had prepared thoroughly what she wanted to say she was convinced that she would never ever be able to stand before a large audience and actually **say** it.

Lying there, restless, sleepless, her previous life swept vividly before her... As though it had been in a film. Up on a screen...

As a child of four. Her aunt coming to her with the grim news, "Your mother has died. A lady will be coming to take you to a Children's Home." Her brother and she were to be split up. He was going to one Home, she to another.

When 'the lady', Miss Joblin, a social worker, came to take Nora away, she refused to get into the car. However, with a combination of gentle persuasion and not so gentle pushing from Miss J. she was forced into it. Then, riding along in the back of that Austin Seven, she decided that now she was in the car she wasn't going to get out of it for anybody. At any Children's Home... So when they eventually arrived at Nora's 'new home' she flatly refused to budge. She wasn't leaving the car.

Taking a tight grip of the edge of the back seat with her tiny hands she yelled out in defiance, "No! No! No!"

Persuasion, gentle or otherwise, wouldn't work this time. The stern Miss Joblin sensed that in sixty seconds. She had seen it all before. So she physically dragged her spirited little four year old charge out of the car, screaming and kicking, up the path. And left her, not screaming now, but sobbing softly, in the first of the two Children's Homes where she was to live for the next few months before being allocated to a foster home.

The next image on her mental screen was of a night in Liverpool. In a boxing arena. As a girl of seventeen. The time when she realized that somebody, called God, actually loved her. And she trusted in Him, and was converted.

One by one the pictures flashed through.

Meeting Eddie. The wedding in Caldbeck. The birth of the children. The lorries and the spreaders, coming and going at Newlands Hill. They were all there. In one rapidly rolling kaleidoscope. The pattern of a life. Every image different, but a part of the one before.

Then there came a very graphic recollection of the night when she nearly died. As a young mother, with small children. In the early 1960's...

On that day, Eddie had received a message at work. 'Get home as fast as ever you can! Nora's very ill!' When he arrived home in haste he discovered that the message he had been given had been right. She was. Suddenly. Inexplicably. Very ill.

A doctor was called, and on examining his patient, he had her rushed by ambulance to hospital in Carlisle.

As Eddie watched the ambulance race off, carrying his dangerously ill wife to hospital, the family doctor was preparing to leave. He moved up beside the distraught husband and whispered, "I just think you should know, Eddie. I don't think Nora will see the morning."

Eddie went into the hospital to see her. And then returned home to pray. It was all he could do.

Nora lay in that hospital bed. Feeling extremely weak and ill.

She prayed too. It was a cry of anguish from the heart of a mother.

"Please God, I don't want to die," she pleaded. "I want to go home to Eddie and the children."

Then, during that night of illness, with doctors and nurses padding furtively and frequently in and out, Nora realized something. It was a revelation from God. About His expectations for her life. God wanted her will as well as her heart. He wanted her to surrender her life to Him. To be ready for action. As an instrument for Him to use. In His service. In His will. In His time.

That night, in her extreme weakness, Nora vowed, "Lord, if I live, I will serve You. Wherever and however You want."

By next morning nothing short of a miracle had occurred.

Nora's sickness was completely gone.

Her doctors were completely flabbergasted.

The hospital phoned Eddie to ask him if he would like to come in and take his wife home!

Now here she was. Lying in a well-appointed hotel bedroom, nearly thirty years later, worried sick about standing up and speaking for God. Had she not said that she would do whatever He wanted? Wherever it was.

Throughout the wakeful watches of the night He had been reminding her of His goodness to her. Where He had brought her from. The position He had brought her into.

And that promise to Him...

Nora slipped out of bed, onto her knees. At four o 'clock in the morning. And began to pray, and pray, and pray... For help, and strength, and guidance.

Rising from her knees to sit on a bedside chair, she reached for her Bible and began to read. The Psalm she turned to was one she had been thinking about some weeks previously.

There in that bedroom, as the light of an early summer morning slowly filtered through the curtains, it came back to her with an alarming freshness. After a totally sleepless night.

It was Psalm 121. The third and fourth verses struck home to her heart. They seemed to be just for her.

'He will not suffer thy foot to be moved: he that keepeth thee will not slumber.

Behold, he that keepeth Israel shall neither slumber nor sleep.'

Gradually it dawned upon her. A fresh appreciation of something which she had often read, and even spoken to others about. Something she would have claimed to have known.

"I have been awake all night. Nervous. Anxious. Ready to quit. Yet God has been looking after me. Revealing Himself to me, and guiding me to this point. He isn't asleep. And He doesn't sleep. He will not allow 'my foot to be moved'. I won't slip, or falter, or fall, if I go forward with Him...

At that moment of realization Nora received wonderful assurance.

She climbed back into bed and slept for soundly for all that was left of the night!

Then next day she went on to the Convention platform and delivered her message, possibly not brimming over with confidence, but certainly not choked with fear, either. Having prayed virtually ceaselessly beforehand for guidance in the matter, she gave a simple but sincere word of exhortation.

This proved to be a blessing and benefit to many.

Not least, herself!

34

THERE'S NOTHING IN
YOUR HEAD, MR. STOBART!

❖

During that first year of Nora's chaplaincy of the Auxiliaries, her faith and trust in God were severely tested. For in that year Eddie became suddenly seriously ill. It was alarming. And it happened in the cold days and dark nights of approaching winter.

The annual election of office-bearers in the West Cumbrian branch of The Gideons was scheduled to take place on Friday 29th November, 1991, and since an independent chairman was required for such a meeting, Eddie had been invited to attend and perform that function. This was nothing new for him. He had done it often.

As he and Nora were having tea with a couple from the Branch, before the meeting, Eddie began to feel sick. And dizzy.

When it came the appointed time, Eddie went along to the meeting with the others. He found it difficult, though. Not wanting to let anyone know just how miserable he felt, yet not wanting to stand up for any length of time either, for if he did he was sure that he would fall, Eddie said that he 'hadn't been feeling too great this last couple of days'. And remained firmly in his seat. Even with that the room seemed to start revolving around him. Concentrating on what he was saying became almost impossible. Great waves of nausea swept over him.

Having conducted the business of the meeting as quickly and efficiently as possible in the circumstances, Eddie and Nora set off for home. All Eddie wanted to do was lie flat in bed and hope that his world would stop spinning around him.

They had only gone a few miles along the road, however, when Eddie realized that he couldn't drive any further. It was out of the question. He felt so weak and totally disorientated. The glare of the lights of oncoming vehicles and the pitch darkness of winter-still country roads all flashed past in one big endless blur of black and white.

It was madness for him to be behind the wheel.

So he handed over to Nora, who drove home.

When they arrived outside their bungalow, Eddie struggled out of the car and by a combination of crawling along the floor and sliding along the walls, reached the bedroom.

What a relief it was to roll into bed! To lie flat. At least he wouldn't feel so sick if he could lie down. Perhaps he might feel better in the morning.

That was not to be the case, however.

Next morning Eddie was nothing better. But had rather grown worse. He couldn't stand, at all. Couldn't so much as put a foot to the floor. Couldn't even sit up in the bed without feeling that he was about to fall forward on his face!

So Nora phoned the family doctor, who, when he heard Nora describe her husband's symptoms, attended as soon as possible.

After giving him a thorough examination, the doctor made his diagnosis. It was small wonder that he was reluctant to tell it to Nora, for he was sure that she would be shocked by it.

He was right, too.

She was.

"I think Eddie has a brain tumour, Nora," he said, with a controlled sense of urgency. "I want to have him admitted to The Cumberland Infirmary in Carlisle straight away. I will make all the necessary arrangements. Do you want me to call an ambulance?"

"No. No ambulance please, if I can possibly do without it," Eddie requested. Even terrible pain couldn't quench his manly country pride.

Real men rode on tractors and in trucks, not in ambulances, as far as he was concerned.

Not wanting Nora to be saddled with the sole responsibility for taking her by-now-very-ill husband to hospital alone, the doctor phoned Ann and Ken, who, when they learnt of dad's worsening condition came over immediately. They lost no time, either, in transporting him the six miles in to The Cumberland Infirmary.

Eddie's case was critical. So minutes saved could be vital.

Although it was a Saturday, the family G.P. had requested that all the possible tests should be carried out, and a scan arranged, to pin-point the source of his patient's problem. For his condition seemed to be deteriorating, and the pain in his head intensifying, by the hour.

On that Saturday, Edward had just arrived home from Romania, having been away for two weeks, with two wagons, carrying aid. When he heard, on his return, that his father was in The Infirmary he went directly to the hospital.

During the day Eddie had been subjected to all kinds of tests. And examinations. Doctors of all ranks, from junior housemen to consultants, had been talking to him. Then looking in his eyes. Peering in his ears. And banging him on the head with little hammers.

When Edward arrived his dad was just about to be taken away for a scan. Conscious of the fact that he must be very tired, his mum said to him, "Edward if you want to go on home, you can. I will stay for another while, then I will be going home, too. Janette has come over to be with me, and to keep me company overnight, and I don't want to keep her here too long."

Edward had just been to Romania, but he wasn't going anywhere now though. He had matters on his mind.

"We will not be going until we find out the results of the scan," he announced, emphatically. Then he went on, "What's more, I want to have a prayer with dad before I leave."

So there they remained. Mother Nora, son Edward, daughter Ann, son-in-law Ken, and fourteen year-old granddaughter Janette.

They hadn't long to wait for the results, either.

A doctor, known to the family, broke the news to Eddie as he was being wheeled back to the ward.

"You will be pleased to know, Mr. Stobart," he confided, "we think there is nothing there."

Although he was so dizzy that he couldn't walk, so sick that he couldn't eat, and had an almost unbearable pain in his head, Eddie's native wit hadn't deserted him.

"You tell me that you have just found out that there is nothing in my head. I have known that for sixty year!" he retorted, trying hard to manage a laugh.

At home, on Sunday morning, Nora phoned Dr. David Carling, in Lancaster, to let him know that Eddie was ill, and thus would be unable to attend a committee meeting with him on the next day. The Monday.

When Dr. Carling heard of the apparently serious nature of his friend's condition, he said, "I will come up to see him this afternoon."

Sunday brought yet more in-depth examinations in the hospital. Although the medical staff were sure that there was 'nothing in Eddie's head' they wanted to investigate a number of other possibilities. They needed to identify the cause of his perplexing complaint. And soon. For Eddie was still as bad as ever. He was showing no signs of improvement, whatsoever.

Dr. Carling arrived at the hospital in mid-afternoon, as he had promised. When he had exchanged greetings with the visiting family around the bed, and put a series of questions to the man-in-pain in the bed, Dr. Carling said, "I feel I know what is causing this. The condition is rare, but I have seen it once or twice before. I will have a word with some of the medical staff here."

With that he set off to seek out a duty doctor.

Twenty minutes later Nora was going out of the ward, on her way home. She noticed that Dr. Carling was still deep in conversation with a hospital doctor in a side room. He motioned to Nora to wait. There was obviously something which he wanted to tell her.

He soon emerged to let the very-worried wife know what he had been thinking. And had suggested to the staff on the ward.

"I am almost certain that what Eddie has is a very rare type of shingles that affects the inner ear," he explained. "That would account for his loss of balance and the terrible pain. The doctors here are beginning to come to that conclusion also. They will be examining that as a possibility very soon."

When further tests were conducted, Dr. Carling's initial diagnosis proved to be correct.

On Tuesday, a doctor informed Eddie that they had confirmed that his ailment was indeed shingles of the inner ear. And also that he could go home.

Eddie was pleased with both these news items.

Although he wasn't exactly dancing-up-and-down-excited to contemplate the persistent pain of shingles for months, perhaps even years, to come, at least he would know the source of his pain. Living with a positive diagnosis, whatever it is, though perhaps not easy, is certainly easier than not knowing the cause of the complaint. The uncertainty of the past four days had been causing anxiety for everybody.

And he was also extremely pleased to be going home. The man who had spent the greater part of his life in the great outdoors, on fields and farms, with loads and lorries, had hated being restricted in a hospital ward.

Being at home didn't bring a rapid or even complete recovery, though. Progress was slow, and Eddie was left with a permanent hearing loss in his right ear.

A few months later, when this partial deafness was discovered and measured, he was asked if he would like to have a hearing aid.

Eddie replied, "No, I don't think so. Sometimes it can be a blessing not to be able to hear!"

Boxing Day, 1991, was Eddie and Nora's ruby wedding anniversary and a family meal was arranged in a hotel near Ullswater.

Since he found walking difficult, and standing still for any prolonged period even more of a problem, Eddie attended with his two ever-present companions. His wife, whose help he had so much appreciated over the previous forty years, and his walking stick, whose help he had been forced to appreciate over the previous four weeks.

During the early part of 1992, Eddie was unable to do anything for months. He had to be content to rest, and recover. Then, later in the year, when he had recovered sufficiently to go into Carlisle for a few days each week, to resume his few remaining business interests where he had left off, he discovered that he just couldn't keep pace with the rapidly changing world of commerce.

The developments at Kingstown left him dumbfounded.

It was a big change from a few trucks coming and going from Newlands Hill with fertilizer, to hundreds of trucks coming and going from massive stores in Carlisle handling every conceivable manner of merchandise.

Gradually Eddie came to realize that he didn't have the interest in business that once he did. There were other things that he could be doing with his life. Things that could be done in his own time and at his own pace. But important things, for they would be for God and the furtherance of Christian work.

So on 15th December, 1992, he resigned as chairman of Eddie Stobart Ltd..

It wasn't long either, until God showed him the way ahead.

He had, indeed, other things for Eddie to do.

35

BUILD A CHURCH

❖

Now that he had completely retired from business, Eddie began to concentrate upon other concerns.

The first of these took him back in mind to his early experience of life in the country. The changing pattern of work throughout the changing seasons at Bankdale Head. He started to take a more active interest in the work on his son John's farm.

The other matter to which he was soon to devote most of his waking hours was in relation to his involvement with and for the work of the church in Wigton.

Over a number of years the members of the church meeting in Union Street Hall had come to realize that something was going to have to be done with their building. As soon as ever possible. They had been meeting there for over twenty years and in that time, the condition of the hall had deteriorated terribly.

Despite their best efforts at maintenance, major structural changes were urgently needed. The plaster on the walls had begun to peel and at first small, and then gradually larger, chunks of the ceiling had started to cave in around them. The kitchen facilities, if they could even be termed 'facilities', what there were of them, were both outdated and inadequate.

In 1993, when Eddie learnt that an adjoining piece of land was being offered for sale, he made enquiries about it, with a view to renovating and extending their building, at one and the same time.

When he met the District Planning Officer to discuss the feasibility of the proposed project, the Planning Officer indicated that he couldn't envisage there being any objection to the extension idea. Then, however, he set Eddie's mind awhirl with a further suggestion of his own.

"Would you not consider building a new church on a vacant site somewhere in the town?" he asked.

"We would," Eddie was quick to assure him, "but there are no vacant sites in Wigton."

"Are there not indeed?" the Planning Officer retorted, in mock surprise. "I could tell you of at least half-a-dozen!"

This he then proceeded to do.

Having discussed it with other church members, Eddie, Nora and Ken set out one day on a tour of all the sites that the Planning Officer had told Eddie about. They hadn't ever realized that there were so many, mostly private, sites available.

Most of the locations had their advantages, but their disadvantages as well. There was one site, though, that seemed to be suitable to their needs in almost every respect.

It was on Low Moor Road, close to the heart of the town and in a well-populated area. Since it was so central it would be easily reached by most of the townsfolk, even on foot. All three agreed that it was an ideal site on which to erect a church building.

After a period of prayer and consideration of the financial commitment required for such a venture, outline planning permission was applied for, and granted, in 1994.

The site was then procured, and building work on the new church, financed by the Low Moor Church Trust, began on 1st August, 1995.

For the next two years Eddie travelled back and forward to that site almost daily. He spent his days watching a new church building take shape from its foundations and consulting with contractors of different types about the minor alterations of plan or unexpected problems that arose from time to time.

As he drove the nine miles from his home to the site in Wigton, Eddie often had a quiet chuckle to himself. He was recalling a well-remembered incident from his childhood. Something which had happened about sixty years previously...

It was a Sunday afternoon at Bankdale Head.

Eddie Stobart was just seven years old. His mother was ill, and since her recovery was expected to take a number of months, his Aunt Hannah had come to care for the family.

Aunt Hannah was a good woman. Sincere but stern.

Aunt Hannah had strict views about Sunday observance, too. Very strict.

If you could do it on a Saturday or a Monday, you didn't do it on a Sunday. Ever. Full stop. Simple as that. You didn't clean your shoes or prepare the vegetables. And if you just happened to be a child you couldn't be seen to be enjoying yourself outside, at all.

Laugh and play on the Lord's Day. No way!

On that particular afternoon young Eddie was playing away with his building bricks on a mat in front of the black-leaded range, quite happily.

Father in an armchair on one side of him. Aunt Hannah in an armchair on the other.

Only Aunt Hannah was paying any attention to Eddie's activities, however. John Stobart's face was completely obscured by 'The Christian Herald' which he was holding up to read by the light from a tiny window.

Probably afraid that the little lad might just be happy and content with his building projects on a 'Sabbath' afternoon, Aunt Hannah couldn't help confronting her inattentive brother with what she considered to be his 'duty' as a Christian parent.

"John, do you think it is right that this boy should be playing with these bricks on a Sunday afternoon?" she enquired, with the air of someone fearing an imminent visitation of fire and brimstone to blow Bankdale Head to bits.

No response.

Total silence.

'The Christian Herald' never moved.

"John, do you think that it is right that this boy should be playing with these bricks on a Sunday afternoon?" she repeated much more aggressively. Brother John's apparent lack of concern about a matter of such grave importance had added an edge of urgency to her enquiry.

This time 'The Christian Herald' did move. Upwards.

John Stobart peered out from beneath it. Impatiently.

He had been right in the middle of an absorbing article.

"Eddie, what are you building?" he asked his block-building son.

" I'm building a house," young Eddie replied, innocently.

"Build a church," was his father's next, and only comment. He lowered 'The Christian Herald' to cover his face. Then continued to read in silence. Subject closed.

"Build a church," he had advised.

More than half-a-century later Eddie was trying his best to help do just that!

36

YOU DON'T HAVE TO SAY ANYTHING

❖

Since her election in 1991, Nora had acted as Chaplain to the Auxiliaries for three years, and then at the Annual Convention in 1994, she was appointed Vice-President. She had held this office for two years when she was approached again by a number of her friends.

"We would like to put your name forward for President, Nora," they said. "It is not only us, either, many others have suggested to us that you are the right person for the position."

Nora felt rather humble, and yet in another sense, honoured, by their approach. She was cautious, nonetheless. Having by then had five years experience as a senior office-bearer in the movement, Nora thanked them for the confidence that they, and others, seemed to place in her, and promised to give the matter prayerful and careful consideration, much as she had done on the two previous occasions when she had been approached.

After some thought she decided to allow herself to be nominated for the highest post in the Auxiliaries, that of President.

In May, 1996, it was Convention time again, and there Nora's nomination was accepted, unopposed, and she was declared elected.

As she had done, immediately following her first appointment as chaplain, Nora began to wonder how she would cope with the pressures of her new position. As chaplain she had spoken at smaller meetings of the Auxiliaries, but now as President she would be expected to address the whole Convention. An audience of perhaps eight hundred people!

After her election Nora began to reflect, with a feeling of mild amusement, upon the night when she had first joined the Auxiliaries. And the promise which had been made to her then, exactly thirty years before. In 1966.

In that year all the wives of the members of the newly-established North Cumberland branch of The Gideons had been invited along to the chairman's home, to which Mrs. Dalgleish, the then-President of the Auxiliaries had also come, to address the assembled ladies. The idea being that she could encourage at least some of them to become members of the Auxiliaries.

Nora attended that meeting with a number of the other wives. They found Mrs. Dalgleish's talk very informative. Indeed, it was more than that. It was both inspirational and challenging, as well. There appeared to be tremendous opportunities to assist in the distribution of the Scriptures. All the talk about meetings, and particularly participation in meetings, had scared Nora off somewhat, however.

Inwardly she would have loved to have been able to jump up immediately and say, "I'll join!" But she couldn't. She had reservations. So she had begun to make excuses for herself.

How could a busy housewife, like her, with a family of four all at school, be expected to attend all those meetings the good lady was talking about?

Anyway, if she did join she wouldn't be much use to them, for she wouldn't pray in public. And she DEFINITELY would not be speaking in public. Anywhere or at any time. Ever.

That just 'wasn't her'.

Or so she thought!

On voicing these reasons, which Nora had considered to be fairly foolproof excuses, to Mrs. Dalgleish, the older lady had looked at her sincerely, and with genuine understanding. She had probably been in the same position at some time in her life.

"My dear, we are not asking you to do any of those things. You will not be expected to speak in public. All we are doing is asking you to join us. To help with the distribution of Bibles and New Testaments. And our meetings are only once a month so that won't take you away from your family too much, either," she explained.

Nora had been left without excuse. If what Mrs. Dalgleish had said was true, then she would join the Auxiliaries. For despite her initial doubts, she knew that she would enjoy the monthly meeting, and it would be great to cultivate friendships with other local Christian women with a common interest.

So she had been persuaded, and had joined.

For many years, too, what Mrs. Dalgleish had said had been true. Nora had been able to assist in the work of the Auxiliaries without addressing public meetings. Local branch meetings had been nothing but informal and enjoyable.

That was years ago.

Now, though, she was in the hands of God. She just committed herself, and the responsibilities of the high office into which He had led the orphan child from Caldbeck, into His hands.

And over the past two years God has led and guided Nora wonderfully as President of the Auxiliaries.

He has enabled her to cope with the pressures of the office.

The travelling. The correspondence. The phone calls from zone representatives from all over the United Kingdom. The Council meetings in Headquarters.

Above all, the one thing she had so much feared. 'The cloud she had so much dreaded'.

Speaking to a capacity crowd at the Annual Convention.

What had been Mrs. Dalgleish's assurance to the new, shy member back in 1966?

"You won't be expected to speak in public."!

Indeed!

37

GONE HOME

❖

John Stobart was beginning to feel his age. He had become conscious of his limitations. One day, when he was in his mid-seven ties, he said to his eldest son, "Eddie, I think I am going to have to give up the preaching."

"Give up the preaching, father," Eddie repeated, rather surprised, for he knew how his father had always loved to present the Gospel. "Why that? Why have you come to that decision all of a sudden?"

"Oh I didn't come to the decision all that suddenly," old John went on. "I have realized for some time that my mind isn't as clear as it used to be." Then he added, with an impish smile, "But last Sunday was the last straw."

"Last Sunday? What happened last Sunday, father?" Eddie asked. He was more curious than ever now.

"Last Sunday, in chapel," his father continued, grinning broadly, " I got Zacchaeus up the tree. And then brought Nicodemus down!"

The old man laughed heartily at what had been his own mistake. Embarrassing at the time, but funny now.

When he had sobered up sufficiently to speak again, he concluded his explanation with a question, "Do you not agree with me that it is about time I gave up?"

Eddie laughed with him. And also agreed with him.

Perhaps it would be a wise idea to cut back on his speaking commitments, now that he was past his 'three score years and ten'.

Although John Stobart then began to curtail his preaching engagements, and failing health in later years prevented him from attending church as he once had done, he continued to take an active interest in Christian work in general in Cumbria, until he passed away in Midtown Residential Home in Caldbeck on 22nd October, 1997.

The large congregation who attended his funeral service in the local Parish Church, three days later, bore testimony to the high regard in which he had been held amongst the members of the rural community amongst whom he had lived.

He had gone home to his reward.

At ninety-four.

A few months prior to her father-in-law's death Nora was upset to learn that her friend Jackie was seriously ill. Jackie, who was by-then a never-miss member of the by-then regular monthly Bible study group had been on holiday in May 1997, and had felt unwell.

Tests carried out on her return home had revealed that she had terminal cancer.

As the illness gradually took hold upon her body in the latter months of that year, Jackie was increasingly in pain. Days became difficult. Long nights even worse.

Despite her constant discomfort, however, Jackie never lost her joy. Her faith in God never wavered. She was an example and inspiration to all those with whom she came in contact. Many friends and former business acquaintances came to visit her during her debilitating illness and if she was at all well enough she spoke to each of them about her Lord. She told them of how she had come to learn about Him through reading her treasured Gideon New Testament, and the Bible studies in Nora's home, and how she had come to trust in Him as her Saviour at the rally in Carlisle.

Her witness was clear and consistent.

Friendly but fearless.

When she was invited to the official opening of the new Low Moor Road Church in November, Jackie determined to be present if she was well enough to be out.

Although very weak, and in constant pain, she attended the opening ceremony that afternoon. It was to be her last outing with her husband.

Jackie was so delighted to be able to be there. Just to be in the company of others who loved the Saviour as she did herself proved to be a tonic to her. And to see a new church opened for the proclamation of the Gospel in Wigton thrilled her soul.

During the tea interval in late afternoon, she said passionately to Ruth Hill, Rowland's wife, "Oh what would I not give to be able to stand up there on that platform and tell everybody what this little book means to me!"

She had sat all through the afternoon session clutching her precious much-read New Testament. Then just in case Ruth should have been in any doubt as to which book she meant, Jackie held it up for her to see.

Towards the end of that same month, Jackie had the joy of becoming a grandmother. She told her friends that she had prayed that God would allow her to hold a little grandchild in her arms, before He took her home to His.

God had answered that prayer. What a source of solace and satisfaction it was for her to nurse baby Rebecca, even for the few minutes that her failing strength would permit.

How she praised God for that privilege!

As 1997 drew to a close Jackie became very ill and was admitted to the Hospice.

Nora went to see her.

She was pitifully weak.

Just before she left her friend's bedside, for the final time, as it was to turn out, Nora bent over to hear what it was that Jackie was trying to say.

There was no fear, no panic in her voice as she whispered, "I think I will soon slip away, Nora. I will soon be safe in the arms of Jesus."

Those were to be the last words that Nora heard Jackie say. For a few days later she passed away.

Jackie had been correct about the mode of her passing, too.

She slipped quietly away, as she had predicted she would.

And she had been absolutely right about her destination, as well.

She went straight into the arms of Jesus, as she had been so confident that she would.

The Salvation Army Citadel in Carlisle was packed, crammed, for Jackie's funeral service. And nobody there could fail to be touched. There was hardly a dry eye in the building. Big burly men wept openly.

Jackie had chosen the hymns for that funeral service herself, and as the capacity crowd sang, as best they could through their tears,

'Be still, for the presence of the Lord,
The Holy One is here',

nobody had to tell them that it was true.

Everybody, including many who hadn't been in a church building for years, knew that. They were conscious of an uncanny sense of the power and presence of God in that funeral service on that tragic-for-the-family-and-friends but triumphant-for-Jackie morning.

In the course of his address the Salvation Army Captain remarked, "Carlisle has today lost a jewel."

It was true.

Jackie, too, had gone home to be with the Lord.

To become, herself, one of His jewels.

At fifty-one.

38

LOOKING BACKWARD, MOVING FORWARD

❖

The early days of November, 1997, were filled with hectic activity for Eddie and Nora Stobart and the members of The Low Moor Church Trust. After a number of postponements, the date for the official opening of the new church had been set for the middle of the month.

Although the target date had been agreed the members of the Trust were aware that the building was by no means ready to be declared open! There were so many finishing touches to be attended to. The tarmac around the building hadn't been laid. The kitchen hadn't been fitted out. All the furniture hadn't arrived.

However, after many urgent phone calls, numerous consultations with the suppliers and contractors, the church was at last declared completed. Ready to be officially opened.

So, on Saturday, 15th November, 1997, after more than three years of planning and prayer, Monday site meetings with the architect and builders, occasional hitches and minor alterations, the Low Moor Road Evangelical Church was about to open its doors to the public.

The first of the two meetings of that memorable day was in the afternoon, and the new church was full. Nearly four hundred people had crowded into the spacious main auditorium and a minor hall. All those who had been involved in any way in the erection of the building had been invited, and many of the townsfolk, who had also all been invited through the press, came out of curiosity.

At that service, Rev. James Mc Callen, General Secretary of London City Mission, and formerly of Carlisle, explained the purpose of the church in and for the community. It was, as defined on the plaque in the hallway, dedicated to 'the preaching and teaching of the Word of God'.

The provision of tea for four hundred people tested both the organizational capacity of the ladies of the church, and the performance under pressure of the brand new kitchen equipment to the utmost. It was, despite the challenge of the large crowd, a very happy relaxed occasion, a time for the renewing of old acquaintances, having a laugh over the now-behind-them problems of the recent past, and looking to the future.

The evening session was a less formal, more family affair.

Eddie gave an interesting outline of the history of the formation of the church. He told of the tent meetings at Newlands and the need to do 'something on Sunday mornings'. He recounted the story of the purchase of the former premises in Union Street and the almost thirty years of meetings in that building. Then, to bring his talk bang up to date, he told of the vision for a new centre 'dedicated to the preaching and teaching of the Word of God' in the district, and the erection of the building in which they were all now so comfortably seated.

Peter Stobart, Eddie's nephew, and his wife Helen, sang two pieces, and Janette, now twenty-one, read out a poem which she had composed highlighting quite graphically the difference between the former premises in Union Street and the new modern building. And the challenge facing the new church in the town of Wigton in years to come.

She had entitled it appropriately, 'Old Yet Ever New.'

With spiders in the sink and damp on the wall,
The heating on the blink, and just to top it all
There's some plasterboard loose, the ceiling falls in,
The hall's full of dust and there's a bird in the kitchen!
We've had our ups and downs, but through it all
We've had some right good times in Union Street Hall.

And the time has come for this Church to move house,
A new step, a big challenge, with no time to drowse.
We're leaving a building behind, not a church,
The Church is the people, the building the perch.
It's an open opportunity to spread further the Gospel.
A bigger building, bigger rooms, and more chairs to fill.

We're surrounded by a needy town
Full of needy people, with lives broken down.
There's work to be done, there are souls to be won.
There are goals to be set, and needs to be met.

And although we don't know what the future may hold
We need to trust in the One who has it all controlled.
We need to stand up boldly, though our numbers be few,
To move out from the old and step into the new.

Unless the Lord is the builder, the Church has no future or gain,
And the labourers labour, but it will oft be in vain,
Christ must be our foundation, the rock upon which we stand,
He must be our chief corner stone, for he holds us in His hand.

So as we try to build the Church up, we need to encourage each
other.
We need to build each other up and share our burdens together.
As we look to the future we must keep pressing on,
We must help each other, spurring each other on.
May God dwell among us, and may we let Him have His way,
As we pray He will guide us and keep us as we trust and obey.

And finally, as we make our abode,
In this new Church building on Low Moor road,
Let us not get diverted, but rather let's keep our focus
Both now and always, firmly fixed on Jesus.

As Eddie and Nora sat there in that service that evening, he on the
platform, she in the congregation, though apart in body they were united
in spirit.

While Janette read her poem they couldn't help but feel pleased with her, but then they reflected that she was only one of twelve very special grandchildren with whom God had blessed them over the previous twenty five years. And they had just recently become great grandparents too!

They had so much for which to praise God.

Sitting there, as the meeting progressed, Eddie thought of his early days at home. His father's preaching and his mother's consistent Christian witness. His conversion, and early days in business. How he and Nora had met, and married, and the blessings of married life and a family of four...

Nora, in turn reflected upon a not-just-quite so happy early childhood. Her conversion in Liverpool and how she had met Eddie. God's healing in sickness, and the rearing of the family. And now her position as President of the Auxiliaries...

Then, as each of them looked around at the church building in which they were sitting, they thanked God for the way in which He had guided them from the annual tent at Newlands to a modern building on Low Moor Road. They praised God also for their many Christian friends, and particularly their co-workers in the present church, without whose help that day would never have taken place.

The materials used in the construction of that new building and the furnishings and equipment in it were of the highest possible quality, for in that, as in every aspect of their lives, Eddie and Nora had insisted that 'only the best will do'.

For in this instance it was different from many of their former-life situations and decisions. It was even more special.

It wasn't just a case of 'only the best will do' for Eddie and Nora.

It was only 'the best will do' for God.

The God who had led, guided, and protected them throughout their lives, and in the first instance had given the best He had, His only Son, for them.

APPENDIX

Many people who have seen the Eddie Stobart Ltd. trucks on the trunk roads and motorways of Britain will be interested in the following factfile, updated in October 1998:-

- The company now employs 2,000 staff of whom 1,100 are the drivers.
- Eddie Stobart Ltd. is Britain's largest independent road haulier with more than 700 trucks and over 1,200 trailers on the road.
- Each Eddie Stobart Ltd. truck has a girl's name painted on the cab. The first lorry to be named was 'Twiggy', in 1976.
- The company maintains over 4,000,000 square feet of warehousing space.
- There are 17 strategically located Eddie Stobart Ltd. depots throughout Britain. The most northerly of these is in Glasgow, Scotland, and the most southerly Poole in Dorset.
- The approximate total fuel consumption of all Eddie Stobart Ltd. vehicles for the past year was 10,000,000 gallons.
- Each Eddie Stobart Ltd. truck is fitted with a band 3 radio and modern satellite tracking keeps an accurate record of over 3,000 movements a day.
- Twelve years ago Edward and William Stobart decided to 'go for it big'.
- The two regional centres at Carlisle in the north and Daventry in the south are manned 24 hours a day, 365 days in the year.
- Radio data terminals are fitted to all Eddie Stobart Ltd. fork lift trucks and handsets are operated in all warehouses. This system allows the exact location of every pallet, whether in a warehouse or on a truck, to be pinpointed at any time of the day or night.
- The approximate total mileage covered by Eddie Stobart Ltd. trucks in the past year was 88,000,000 miles. (To put that distance in an understandable perspective - It is approximately the same distance as 3,500 times around the Equator or 160 times to the Moon and back!)

The publishers would like to thank the management of Eddie Stobart Ltd. for their co-operation in the compilation of the above factfile and the production of this book.

OTHER BOOKS BY THE SAME AUTHOR

MY FATHER'S HAND

THIS IS FOR REAL

JUST THE WAY I AM

SOME PARTY IN HEAVEN

FIRST CITIZEN SMYTH

SOMETHING WORTH LIVING FOR

HOW SWEET THE SOUND

AS OUR HEADS ARE BOWED